Praise for

PRODUCTIVE
RELATIONSHIPS

"Jan Yager combines exhaustive research with sharp thinking and engaging writing to give us a powerful guidebook to navigating the workplace. In these pages you'll meet "vampires," "visionaries," "idea thieves" and "saboteurs." You'll also see yourself, and how your work life can change for the better."

—Jeffrey Zaslow, coauthor,
The Last Lecture and *Highest Duty*

"Especially during times of scarce organizational resources and understandably strained office relationships, everyone could benefit from such sage advice as Jan Yager's."

—Lily Garcia, columnist for the *Washington Post*,
human resources consultant, and employment attorney

"I highly recommend reading Jan Yager's new book, *Productive Relationships.* Yager's savvy and practical guide breaks it all down for you so you gain dozens of insightful strategies and skills to succeed with 'the good, the bad and the ugly' in the workplace."

—Don Gabor, author,
How to Start a Conversation and Make Friends

"*Productive Relationships* is a pleasure to read with tactics that are simple to implement and guaranteed to improve relationships with a boss, a colleague or an intern."

—Cammy Bourcier, Senior VP,
Broadcast and New Media Public Relations

"Read this book and you'll find out how to deal with negative personality types, become more of a team player, listen carefully, make a great first impression, and much, much more. I highly recommend it!"

—Simon T. Bailey, international speaker and author,
Release Your Brilliance

"What a useful book for initiating and strengthening your work or business relationships!"

—Mary Jones, talk show host

PRODUCTIVE
RELATIONSHIPS

SELECTED OTHER BOOKS BY JAN YAGER, PH.D.

Nonfiction

—

Business Protocol: How to Survive & Succeed in Business
Who's That Sitting at My Desk?: Workship, Friendship, or Foe?
Effective Business and Nonfiction Writing
When Friendship Hurts
Friendshifts: The Power of Friendship and How It Shapes Our Lives
Work Less, Do More: The 14-Day Productivity Makeover
Creative Time Management for the New Millennium
Creative Time Management
365 Daily Affirmations for Time Management
365 Daily Affirmations for Creative Weight Management
365 Daily Affirmations for Happiness
125 Ways to Meet the Love of Your Life
Road Signs on Life's Journey
Victims
The Help Book
Career Opportunities in the Film Industry, 2nd ed (with Fred Yager)
Career Opportunities in the Publishing Industry, 2nd ed
(with Fred Yager)

Fiction

—

The Pretty One
Untimely Death (with Fred Yager)
Just Your Everyday People (with Fred Yager)
The Cantaloupe Cat (illustrated by Mitzi Lyman)

PRODUCTIVE RELATIONSHIPS

57 Strategies for Building **Stronger** Business Connections

JAN YAGER, Ph.D.

HANNACROIX CREEK BOOKS, INC.
Stamford, Connecticut

ISBN 978-1-889262-63-5 (hardcover)
Published by:
Hannacroix Creek Books, Inc.
1127 High Ridge Road, #110 Stamford, Connecticut 06905 USA
http://www.hannacroixcreekbooks.com
hannacroix@aol.com

Book Cover & Interior Design by Scribe Freelance | www.scribefreelance.com

---

Library of Congress Cataloging-in-Publication Data

Yager, Jan, 1948-
  Productive relationships : 57 strategies for building stronger business connections / Jan Yager.
      p. cm.
  ISBN 978-1-889262-63-5 (hardcover) — ISBN 978-1-889262-60-4 (trade pbk.)
1. Customer relations—Management. 2. Business communication. 3. Success in business. I. Title.
  HF5415.5.Y33 2011
  650.1'3—dc22
                        2010024026

Contents

● ● ●

Introduction

Brian's supervisor called him the "it" guy. Whatever *it* was that needed doing, Brian was the person she turned to to get the job done. A designer for a global financial services firm, Brian excelled at producing provocative and persuasive visual elements for an array of marketing products. He could design anything and make it stand out, from a motivational recruitment brochure to a dynamic cover for the internal employee magazine. His boss once sent him an unsolicited note in which she called him "the best designer" she had ever worked with.

Then, one day, a restructuring occurred and Brian found himself reporting to a new boss. His latest manager wasn't as open and friendly as his previous superior. Always businesslike and curt, she failed to appreciate Brian's sense of humor and easygoing nature. Brian quickly realized that this new boss was not nearly as enthralled with Brian or his work as his former supervisor had been. And while the assignments were similar to those he had done in the past, suddenly nothing he created was acceptable. After a few weeks of being told his once-admired designs now "needed work" and to "keep trying," he was called into his latest supervisor's office and told he was being let go. "It just isn't working out," she told a somewhat shocked Brian.

He couldn't believe it! How could his work go from being well-regarded to suddenly unacceptable?

The issue wasn't Brian's work at all. Where he always had an open and positive relationship with his previous boss, there now was no rapport and goodwill between Brian and his latest supervisor. Brian hadn't realized in time that he needed to cultivate a warm relationship with this new superior or her perception of his work would suffer. He had taken for granted that his previously well-regarded work would speak for itself. He also assumed that he would automatically enjoy the same strong relationship with this new supervisor that he had with his first boss. If he had at least tried to win her over, would things have turned out differently? Unfortunately, Brian will never know.

IT'S NOT JUST *WHAT* AND *WHO* YOU KNOW— IT'S HOW WELL YOU GET ALONG!

You have probably heard the saying that when it comes to being successful in business, "it's not just what you know, it's who you know." Brian's experience demonstrates a third component: "it's how well you get along." It was Brian's failure to forge a solid relationship with his new supervisor—rather than the quality of his work—that ultimately cost him his job.

To be truly successful in today's business world, you have to be able to navigate the minefield of workplace and business relationships. It is paramount that you learn how to unravel these often complex human interactions if you want to find a job or keep the one you have—let alone, rise to the top. You need to be able to discern the hidden tripwires that could trigger a career-ending verbal exchange. And you must become adept at deciphering the clues that will let you know you've gotten onto the wrong side of office politics. If you are an entrepreneur, or a freelancer, you will still need to know how to get along well with your clients and customers even if you do not find yourself in traditional workplace setting on a daily basis.

Compounding matters in today's workplace are two divergent concepts: a heightened degree of competitiveness, and a greater emphasis on teamwork. Each has specific qualities impacting your ability to build relationships. Organizations that fuel competition often make it difficult for employees to form durable, caring bonds because they find themselves competing against their peers. Still, constructive work connections are precisely what you need to develop in order to survive (and thrive) at work and in business.

On the other hand, with more businesses emphasizing

teamwork, there is an increased likelihood that you could be faced with a 360-degree performance evaluation. You will be judged not only by those above you, but by those below and alongside you as well. Relationship-building now has turned into an even more complicated endeavor as you are pressured to connect positively in so many directions.

The bottom line: getting along at work and in business, and learning how to deal more effectively with negative or harmful work relationships, is essential to your success, no matter where you are in your career. Consider these circumstances:

- You have been promoted and you wonder if there is a way to maintain the friendships you developed with your former coworkers even though you are now in a supervisory role.
- You think that one of your coworkers is trying to sabotage you, but need help to identify the signs.
- You've felt secure in the job you've held for the last ten years, but recently you were told of impending massive layoffs if enough employees do not take voluntarily early retirement. You don't know what to do next.
- You have already lost your job and need to network more than ever before, and more effectively, to find a new position in a very tough job market.
- You just landed a new job and you need to learn how to build positive work relationships—and fast!—in order to hit the ground running at this company.

This book will teach you how to engage your co-workers and learn about what's going on in their lives, since sensitivity to others affects your career. It also will provide direction if you feel your career has stalled or derailed; show you how to develop a stronger allegiance to your co-workers; give you tips on how to get along better with your boss; and guide you toward creating a more positive work environment. You will learn, too, how to build a more loyal professional network, and how to find a mentor or colleagues who will support your professional growth. Other vital topics discussed in this book will help you learn how to:

- Improve your listening skills at work
- Cultivate advocates who will write strong and praiseworthy recommendation letters on your behalf
- Find and befriend the movers and shakers at your company and in your industry
- Deal effectively with a coworker who has been gossiping about you behind your back
- Examine how body language impacts on work relationships
- Explore 13 key positive and 15 negative types you may encounter at work, why someone might be that way, and how to best deal with him or her
- Find or create your own Mastermind or professional support group so you continue to grow your business or career knowledge and networks
- Avoid conflict, or resolve disagreements that are unavoidable
- Use those time-consuming meetings to strengthen relationships
- Circumvent the perils of workplace technology that can be negatively impacting on your work relationships, such as overuse of e-mail in lieu of phone calls or face-to-face meetings

Productive Relationships is based on scores of interviews with men and women in various stages of their careers, business and career experts, as well as my own diverse first-hand experiences in the workplace and in business including working for the legendary publishing executive, Barney Rosset, and the Pulitzer Prize-winning author, Norman Mailer. Beginning with my fulltime jobs in my teens, including working as the assistant to the head of the outpatient clinic at Bellevue Hospital, over the years, I have worked for and with a wide range of co-workers, bosses, and academic department chairs. Those experiences have helped me to personally appreciate, and to observe in others, the power of positive work relationships as well as the harm negative relationships can have on our lives, our careers, and even our self-esteem and mental and physical health.

One of your first considerations as you begin on your road to better mastery of your workplace and business relationships is to figure out where you stand in those relationships right now. Please take a few moments out of your busy day to take the quiz that follows to find out. It will provide you with a valuable starting point for your interpersonal connections, including how well you are currently getting along with your boss, co-workers, subordinates, and even customers and clients. (Please note: if this is a library book, you could write your answers on a separate piece of paper, instead of in the book, or, if you prefer, you could photocopy the self-inventory and write on that copy.)

OFFICE OR BUSINESS RELATIONSHIP SELF-INVENTORY

1. Jot down the name of each individual that is key to your business success—coworker, boss, employee, service provider, client, or customer. For each name, ask yourself: "Is our relationship good? Excellent? Or is it negative and potentially damaging? Could it use improvement?" Make a note of your answers.

———————————————————————————

———————————————————————————

———————————————————————————

———————————————————————————

———————————————————————————

2. Study that list, because it is telling you which relationships/individuals you need to cultivate. Prioritize who you will start with, and use this book to work on developing a plan to improve that relationship.

3. How wide is your business network at work? in your industry? at any of the social media networking sites that you belong to? Write down the number of contacts that you have at each site that you currently belong to, such as linkedin.com, xing.com, facebook.com, classmates.com, or plaxo.com.

SOCIAL MEDIA SITE	NUMBER OF CONTACTS
Linkedin.com	_____
Facebook.com	_____
Classmates.com	_____
Xing.com	_____
Plaxo.com	_____
Myspace.com	_____
Other (fill in) _____	_____

4. If you want to expand your social online or in-person networks, how do you want to expand it? Have you identified those individuals that you wish to meet and try to get to know? If not, take the time to make a "wish list" of potential new contacts or reconnections right now.

WISH LIST FOR NEW CONTACTS OR RECONNECTIONS

Name	Type of contact:	
	New	Reconnect
_____	_____	_____
_____	_____	_____
_____	_____	_____
_____	_____	_____
_____	_____	_____

_____	_____ _____
_____	_____ _____
_____	_____ _____
_____	_____ _____
_____	_____ _____

5. Do you know who the movers and shakers are in your company or in your industry? Have you selected those with whom you would like to be on a first-name basis? Write down those names and how you might possibly meet, or get introduced to, those individuals.

MOVERS AND SHAKERS IN MY COMPANY (OR INDUSTRY)

Name   Who will I meet/connect with? How will we connect?

_____

_____

_____

_____

_____

6. How many hours a week do you spend calling your current or previous coworkers, or going out to lunch or for a drink or dinner after work, to catch up and find out what's new?

TIME SPENT WEEKLY CONNECTING WITH
CURRENT/PREVIOUS COWORKERS

Name of Coworker   Time Spent   Type of Activity

_____

_____

_____

_____

_____

8. Do you have a network of at least 50 to 100+ people who know you at your current or previous jobs and to whom you could turn for leads, recommendations, or just support if you were to lose your job today? Make a list of your current network with the goal of expanding to 50 to 100 *strong* and *positive* business connections who care about you and who want to help you to succeed.

9. If you were to get promoted today, or find out you won a coveted award, is there at least one person at work, or in your business, with whom you could share the good news and who would be genuinely happy for you?

10. Have you ever wondered if you should take a course on getting along better at work?

11. Has anyone ever told you that you should take an anger management class?

12. What are your relationship goals for your job or for your business?

13. Do you prefer to keep your business and your personal relationships separate?

14. Do you think conflict at work should always be avoided? If you were to find yourself in an unavoidable workplace conflict, do you have a mastery of conflict resolution techniques that could help you get through it?

15. If someone managed to bring a weapon into your office, would you know the recommended way to exit without confronting the intruder, or another way to decrease the likelihood that you would be confronted?

16. How comfortable are you working with someone who is a generation older or younger than you are?

Comfortable _____ Uncomfortable _____

17. If you work with or for someone from another culture, or if you conduct business in another country, have you taken the time to understand some of the key concerns that you may have to address in your business relationships? These might include language, dress, appropriate personal space, gift giving, gift acceptance, or attitudes toward work relationships. Use the space below to consider some of the cultural similarities or differences that you need to address at work or in your business relationships over the phone or through e-mail:

_____

_____

_____

_____

_____

18. Have you considered how your childhood or previous job relationships (even part-time or summer employment) could be impacting how you handle current situations, or allow yourself to be treated, at work or in business today? Use the space below to write about your previous work relationships, the good, the bad, and the ugly.

_____

_____

_____

_____

_____

19. Have you ever had one coworker who was particularly memorable? What made him or her so unforgettable?

_____

_____

_____

_____

_____

20. If you were to describe your ideal work or business relationship, what would it be like?

_____

_____

_____

_____

_____

Now that you have taken this office/business work relationships self-inventory, you have a starting point for evaluating your current office or business relationships. The information, examples, and anecdotes throughout this book will help you reconsider or reexamine your answers to the previous twenty questions.

But remember that you are recording your experiences and opinions *at this one point in time.* Make note of when you took this self-quiz and then return to it whenever your workplace relationships or circumstances change—for example, you get a new coworker, boss, or customer, you get a new job, you switch careers, or you go from employment to self-employment.

Improving your workplace relationships is a journey that is ongoing based on new knowledge and fresh experiences. Therefore, in the last chapter of this book, you'll have a chance to retake the twenty-question work relationship self-inventory that you just took but that time it will be to help you assess your progress, and also to solidify your goals for the future.

Over the years, I've worked for, or with, some amazing leaders and administrators, as well as with those who were really tough to get along with and from whom it was sometimes very hard to recover when the work ended. Still, I learned a lot about workplace and business relationships from every job experience, especially from those that *didn't* work out.

Most of us spend more time at our work than we do with just about anything or anyone else in our lives. Because of that reality, we might as well make it more enjoyable and more productive by learning to seek out and strengthen the positive work relationships that come our way as well as how to deal more effectively with the annoying ones that are unavoidable.

Happy reading!

Chapter One

In the Blink of an Eye: Positive First Impressions for Fostering Business Connections

Strategy #1
Use Body Language That Welcomes Relating

Albert Mehrabian's research studies on how we decide we like someone has led to these generalizations: just 7% of how we judge someone is verbal. The rest is through tone of voice (33%), and through general body language (55%).

These statistics, even if somewhat distorted in meaning through the simplification process, still point out a key consideration for all of us: avoid over-relying on any one type of communication. This is especially important to emphasize with easy and free e-mail, which at times seems to be replacing the telephone and the in-person get-together for business interactions.

The value of studying body language has been thrust into the spotlight with the 2009 premiere of the U.S.-based TV show called "Lie to Me." At first the show seemed a bit awkward and forced as the main character, Dr. Cal Lightman, played by Tim Roth, based on the real-life clinical psychologist and body language expert Paul Ekman, Ph.D., looked at every single grimace or eyebrow twitch as a way to determine whether a suspect was lying, fearful, defensive, or embarrassed. But soon the cases he was working on became very compelling, and were made all the more provocative by the plot's emphasis on body language.

For example, current characters' facial expressions are compared to similar ones gathered from throughout history in the guise of photos of famous and infamous world figures which are flashed on a screen. The TV show provides a dramatic example of the body language that we all need to become aware of and adept at reading to help us triumph in our workplace relationships and thus, our careers.

That is why an overemphasis on just e-mail, no matter how efficient it might be, eliminates an avenue for obtaining the valuable information that talking in person or over the phone, provides. Putting a smiley or smiling face in an e-mail, or even writing LOL (Laugh Out Loud), is no substitute for experiencing the real thing, first hand.

FACIAL EXPRESSIONS

Facial expressions are a key component of body language. How good are you at having your facial expressions match the emotion you want to convey? You definitely want to have consistency in your facial expressions and your words or you could get a reputation for being a phony, or even a liar, if you face says one thing and your words say another. For example, someone asks you, "What do you think of the new design?" and you blurt out, "Terrific!" but your face is all squished up and you look conflicted and upset rather than enthusiastic.

Conversely, in a business setting, if it is politically correct to give one kind of response even if you are thinking another one, are you good at concealing your emotions so that you do not give away your contradictory thoughts? Perhaps you are looking for a job—you have made up your mind that you need to leave this job, even this field, and there is nothing anyone could do at your current job to get you to want to stay—but you do not want anyone to know at your current job until you have something else lined up. If someone asks you, "Are you happy working here?" can you say "Yes," and sound as if you mean it since you prefer the atmosphere to be as positive as possible until you make your move?

13

A popular promotional item is a sheet of faces with a magnet on the back that consists of six rows of faces, and each row has a head with five different facial expressions. What you do is move a square over the face that matches the words on the square that reads "Today I feel." The sheet offers thirty possible moods that someone could feel on any given day, ranging from "frustrated," "confident," or "shy," to "bored," "anxious," or "happy." How many of us take the time to figure out how we are really feeling on any given day, and how that impacts the way we interact with others? And what about those we are dealing with; what are they feeling?

Even if we are self-conscious about telling someone our feelings, increased sensitivity at reading non-verbal cues as to how someone feels can only help communication and relationships.

SMILE!

"Let a smile be your umbrella," is a well-known adage. In the workplace, the saying should be, "let a smile be the way you greet and meet if you want people to welcome being around you." That wise sage, Dale Carnegie, put it this way: "Actions speak louder than words, and a smile says, 'I like you. You make me happy. I am glad to see you.'

"That is why dogs make such a hit. They are so glad to see us that they almost jump out of their skins. So, naturally, we are glad to see them.

"An insincere grin? No. That doesn't fool anybody. We know it is mechanical and we resent it. I am talking about a real smile, a heartwarming smile, a smile that comes from within, the kind of smile that will bring a good price in the market place."

GESTURES AND TOUCH (HAPTIC COMMUNICATION)

Gestures include everything from the handshake or the kiss on the cheek (or lips) to the pat on the back, or a tapping or patting on the shoulder to communicate comfort when someone shares something sad or traumatic.

Gestures are especially notable when someone speaks to a group, whether at a departmental meeting or in front of an audience of nine hundred. Are the speaker's hands waving wildly, distracting everyone from the words that are being spoken from the podium, or are the hand gestures a way of emphasizing ideas and concepts?

In everyday speaking situations, gestures can be in the service of what is being said, or gestures can be annoying or in the disservice of the words (especially evident when someone has a problem with fidgeting).

What used to be considered an annoyance (for example, a co-worker inappropriately touching another's shoulder) today could be the beginning of an accusation of sexual harassment. Bottom line: in work-related situations, be very careful about who you touch and where. If someone touches you in a way that you find unpleasant or inappropriate, if you think it's a question of a cultural difference, a mistake, or even someone testing you out to see what, if anything, you will put up with, politely inform this individual that you don't think he or she meant anything by it but you find that kind of touching inappropriate and offensive and you do not want it to happen again. Hopefully this person will get the hint and there will not be a repetition of the unpleasant touching. If you think your workplace does not have clear enough guidelines about this, you might suggest to human resources that they have a lawyer or human resource/sexual harassment expert offer a workshop on the topic, or show an educational video that addresses these issues. Or, the human resources department could pass around a handout or more extensive literature that details what is and is not appropriate in the workplace, and spell out what kinds of touching could be seen as signs of sexual harassment (even if it was not meant to be seen that way).

POSTURE OR BODY POSITIONING
(PROXEMIC COMMUNICATION)

Another aspect of body language that conveys a first impression is your posture. Augusta Nash, a coach based in Atlanta, has trained on body language with the Newfield Network. Says Nash, "They teach you that your body language and your mood have to be aligned for people to trust you."

Nash also points out that there are posture considerations appropriate to the role that someone plays at work. For example, you expect the leader (the boss) to "stand up straight as well as having peripheral vision, the ability to see in all directions."

Do you want to convey authority and confidence? Stand up straight and tall. Do you want to be seen as youthful and energetic, even if you are sixty or older? Avoid hunching over, which is the type of posture you will sadly see too often in a nursing home. Do you want to be seen as engaged and engaging? Avoid standing with your arms crossed, which conveys defensiveness and being distant.

PERSONAL SPACE

Edward Hall is a renowned anthropologist who has explored personal space across cultures. In his classic works, *The Silent Language* and *The Hidden Dimension*, he notes that there are clear cultural distinctions in how much personal space is appropriate and necessary. While there is no right or wrong when it comes to personal space, the key is in knowing what is comfortable based on the culture (or country) that you are in, and even what kind of personality you are dealing with. Some people can tolerate, or even need, more distance than others when they communicate face to face.

Ask yourself these questions to better understand your own needs for personal space:

- How far away from someone do you need to be to feel comfortable in a business setting?
- What would you do if someone moved too close to you and you prefer to be further away? How would you handle it?
- Do you work with those from other cultures, or do you travel internationally, where the personal space needs are dramatically different from your own? What are those differences? (For more on this, see Strategy #44 in Chapter 7.)

The Non-Verbal Aspects of Language

Another part of body language is the *pace* with which you speak. I once interviewed a woman who spoke so quickly that I felt assaulted with her words. It was a personality trait and since she was in her fifties, it was not a trait that she was likely to change any time soon. I wondered if she knew how negatively her speaking speed probably affected most aspects of her professional life. There are classes and workshops that one can attend to improve one's speaking patterns, as well as coaches one can work with to improve the rhythm of speech. Another faster and easier solution, although it may not have as many long-term positive results, is to become aware of this tendency and to find alternative ways of communicating that do not depend on the pace of speaking. For instance, using e-mail communication might be more effective for this individual or for those who share this trait than speaking over the phone or in person.

Word Choice

In addition to pacing are the words that are chosen. Some languages have two words for the same relationship, depending upon whether it is close or professional.

Be careful of your word choice at work or in business settings. If you have the habit of referring to a woman as "Sweetie" or "Dearie," you might want to eliminate that habit so you are not accused of being inappropriate. Slang or curse words are another aspect of language that needs to be addressed. And, be careful about risqué jokes at work and in business, whether you are saying the joke for the first time, repeating it, or simply listening to it—even though you really feel you should excuse yourself when you see where the joke is heading.

Strategy #2
Convey a Positive Attitude

Which of these scenarios is closer to your situation? You go to work everyday. You love your job and the time flies. You would pay them to work there if you had to.

Or, you wonder how you got stuck at this company, and in this situation, and you would like to get a new job, or even switch careers, but it is not a good time to be out of work especially in your industry. You count the minutes till you can punch out, and you dream of someone calling you up and offering you your dream job.

Fortunately, no matter which scenario is closest to your work situation you *can* be cheerful, positive, and a joy to be around at work. If you are self-employed, and you have clients and customers, rather than coworkers and bosses, you can also be positive and engaged and involved in your work in an upbeat way whether this is a dream project or something you took on just for the money.

Your attitude is something you can control. You may not be able to control whether you work at a particular company or whether you get to work on the project of your choosing. But you can be joyful and joyous and you can give yourself permission to find what is positive about a job or a project rather than being negative and focusing on what is disappointing about it, whether it's the salary you're receiving, the people you are forced to be around, or the boss you have to please who never seems to be pleased.

Attitude is from the Italian *attitudine* or *aptitude* or *posture*. *Aptitudo* is from the Latin for *aptus* or *fitness*. We've all heard the expression, "a sound mind and a sound body." Attitude helps us to have a fit mind as we approach situations with a mental fitness that gives us hope, positive energy, and joyfulness, rather than doubt, negativity, and despair. Since attitude is contagious, and since most workplace environments have everyone working in relatively close quarters, why not have joy and positive energy spreading rather than fear, negativity and suspicion.

The suggestions offered by protestant preacher Norman Vincent Peale, author of the bestseller *The Power of Positive Thinking*, first published in 1952, are still relevant today. Peale's book, which has sold millions and has been translated into more than 40 languages, has chapters that expand on these core concepts: Believe in Yourself; A Peaceful Mind Generates Power; How to Create Your Own Happiness; Stop Fuming and Fretting; Expect the Best and Get It; I Don't Believe in Defeat; Break the Worry Habit; Relax for Easy Power; and How to Get People to Like You. While Peale interjects God into many of his thoughts and passages, his advice is sound no matter which God you believe in or even if you are an atheist or an agnostic.

Doug Hensch, COO of a five-person start up, happier.com, shares about how attitude makes a difference: "Loads of research shows that pessimism is bad for us both psychologically and physically. Optimism, on the other hand, has benefits that include higher levels of creativity, longevity, improved health, and much more."

Strategy #3
Present a Pleasant Appearance

What messages do each of us communicate by the clothes we wear, including everything from the jewelry on our fingers or around our necks or wrists, or the earrings in ears, nose, or even eyebrows, to hair ornaments, shoes, the pocketbook or computer bag on our shoulder or that we hold in our hand? What is a coworker who shows up at work in a $400 suit communicating to his peers about his probable socioeconomic status?

Joyce L. Gioia points out how important it is to set standards for dress at work if some employees are failing to exercise good judgment. She shared with me about the challenge of dealing with the dress of one of her employees who had worked for her beginning as a high school intern and then while she was going to college at night. This young employee happened to be an exceedingly attractive former beauty queen. Gioia explains: "Since we never knew when clients were going to show up at our door, at one point, I was personally disturbed by the fact that the men in our organization found her wardrobe distracting. She wore short shorts, tank tops, and often had her midriff showing. We wanted to have a very flexible dress code, and we thought we did. However, we had to draw the line at short shorts, tank tops and bare midriffs. Actually I had the conversation with her myself. I said she was a very beautiful young woman and when she wore clothing like that it was 'unprofessional and distracting to the men'. I added I would appreciate it if she would wear not wear tank tops anymore, wear longer shorts, and make sure that her midriff was covered. Happily, she took it in stride and I no longer had to worry about violations of our dress code."

Strategy #4
Create a Favorable First Impression (In-Person, over the Phone and through E-Mail)

You've heard it before: first impressions count! Remember that you might not get a second chance at this relationship. Take each meeting, e-mail, or phone call seriously. Nothing is inconsequential. It all matters!

Image consultant Camille Lavington believes *You've Only*

Got Three Seconds to make an impression in business (as detailed in her book with the same title). Have you ever called someone on the phone and, within moments, gotten a negative feeling toward the person on the other end of the line because he or she barks at you? You are already starting on the wrong foot, which makes it more difficult, and sometimes nearly impossible, to turn that negativity around.

Even e-mail, though "silent," has the ability to convey a first impression of you, the sender. What you put in the subject line of your communication, how you address the recipient, the content of your message (including how long it is and the tone), and whether or not there are typographical or grammatical errors, or even smileys ☺, will create a first—and often lasting—impression.

Here are some questions to help you determine whether you're making a favorable first impression.

First Impressions: In person
- Is your dress/appearance appropriate for the situation/occasion?
- If a handshake is appropriate, is it a firm grip or too tight?
- Is a kiss an appropriate way to initially greet each other or is that uncomfortable? If a kiss is appropriate, is the style of the kiss consistent with the culture, e.g., one kiss on one cheek in the United States versus a kiss on each cheek in Europe?
- Is your body language warm and welcoming or defensive or aggressive?
- Are names pronounced correctly?
- Did the meeting start on time?
- Is the atmosphere where the meeting takes place appropriate to the business at hand?

First Impressions: Telephone
- Have you done your homework in advance so you know

something about this person as well as his or her company?

- Is your phone equipment in good condition? Some cell phones or portable phones get poor reception; speakerphones may make it hard to hear someone.

First Impressions: E-Mail

- Is your subject line clear and targeted so that you are more likely to have your e-mail opened and read?
- Is the person you are writing to someone you know? If you have been referred by someone, are you explaining that right in the beginning of the e-mail, increasing the likelihood that your e-mail will be valued and responded to promptly?
- Are you sure about the gender of the person to whom you are writing? If you are unsure, are you using the individual's complete name or just the first name, if that is appropriate, so you can avoid having to refer to him or her as Ms. or Mr., which might offend someone if you have the gender wrong.
- Are you keeping your e-mail as short and succinct as possible?
- Have you reread it for sense and clarity, as well as for correcting any typos, fact checking, or making sure any proper names or references are correct?

TELEPHONE ETIQUETTE

If You Are Placing a Call

- Most of us place our phone calls when it is a convenient time for us to talk. The trick, here, is to find out if it is also a useful time for the one you are calling. So ask, "Is this a good time to talk?" or something similar since you are intruding on whatever the person you called is doing.

Don't automatically assume it's a good time to talk just because they happened to answer the phone.

- Set specific goals for this call so you are less likely to ramble or misuse the time. Have a reason for your call even if your reason is to say hello and network.
- Even though it's easier to put someone on speakerphone, proper etiquette requires that you ask permission of the person you are speaking to, beforehand. Also: be mindful that you won't disturb those around you if you are in an open office or cubicle.
- For business calls, stay on point and message. Keep it clear and short. Avoid gong on tangents especially about personal matters.
- Practice pleasant ways to excuse yourself and to end the call that will not alienate or offend the person on the other end.
- Show an interest in the other person without getting too personal.
- Make it clear what the next step will be: will you follow-up with an e-mail, a letter, another call?
- Express your gratitude for the time on the phone.
- Take notes during your phone conversation. Note the time of day that you called, and ask if this is the best time for calling in the future.

If You Are Receiving a Phone Call
- Unless you had set up a phone appointment, it is okay for you to determine if you want to talk to someone at that moment since you did not initiate this call. So if it is not a good time to talk, say that right away. If you let the caller speak too long before you say it, it will sound as if you are cutting him off.
- Even if you are busy or in a bad mood, be pleasant and upbeat.

- Try to determine as quickly as possible who the caller is, why he or she is calling, and whether you are the right person to handle this call.
- If you should not be the one handling this call, suggest someone else, and explain why, and provide that contact information.
- Even if the caller is a total stranger or someone that you are too high-level to be dealing with, be pleasant because you are a reflection on your company or agency.
- Keep an eye on the time without being abrupt.
- Keep a record of who you spoke to and their contact information.

Cell Phone Etiquette
- Turn off your phone, or put it on vibrate, when you are in meetings or situations where it would be intrusive to have it ring.
- When you do answer the phone, be cognizant of who is within earshot. It can potentially violate your privacy, as well as the confidentiality of the person you are speaking to, if others hear one or both sides of your conversation.
- If you are having trouble with reception on your phone, especially if it is an older model, invest the money in a new, updated phone so you don't constantly lose calls or have a hard time hearing when on the line.
- Make sure your cell phone call will not annoy others who are close-by.
- If you are on a train, and there are quiet cars, respect that rule and do not talk on your cell phone in a quiet car. Move to a regular car to talk.
- Politeness counts: if your policy is to deal with business calls only during business hours but you still receive the occasional business call after-hours, still be pleasant, find

out who is calling and why, and ask when you can return the call.

- If you are willing to answer your cell phone at any time, no matter what you are doing, be sure to always answer in a professional way since it could be a business call. If you leave your cell phone number on the voice mail message of your office phone, don't be too surprised or annoyed if someone takes you up on it and does call you on your cell phone. If, when you find out why they called, you disagree that the matter is urgent, calmly and politely figure out how best to handle the call. Avoid getting outraged, angry, or annoyed because someone took the liberty of calling your cell phone.

Strategy #5
Speak in a Friendly Conversational Style

Take this self-quiz to determine what your conversational style is over the phone or in person:

1. What is your preferred way to communicate? In-person? E-mail? Fax? Telephone? Cell phone? Instant message?
2. Do you speak slowly and clearly or do you speak too rapidly to be understood easily?
3. Over the phone, do you find others saying to you, "Could you repeat that?" more than once or twice in a conversation?
4. Do you have an accent that makes you hard to understand?
5. Do you use words that are typical and easy to understand or do you use "big" words that cause others to miss the meaning of what you are saying or to halt the conversation to ask for a definition?

6. Do you have a range of conversational styles, depending upon the purpose of your communication, from informative to persuasive, or do you tend to have the same consistent style?

7. Do you ramble?

8. Do you begin a conversation with a clear idea of what you want to accomplish in this discussion?

9. Do you apply Milo Frank's famous approach, as reflected in his book of the same title, namely do you know *How to Get Your Point Across in 30 Seconds or Less?*

10. Do you end each conversation or meeting with a summary or action plan so there is a shared agreement that your conversation had a clear purpose?

As Frank, who became head of talent and casting for CBS Television, discovered, you can say a lot in just thirty seconds. Frank notes in his classic book, "I've seen careers rise and fall on the spoken word. The employee who can't communicate effectively doesn't get a raise or a promotion. The boss who can't get his point across loses the cooperation of his employees. The salesman who can't stop talking doesn't make the sale..."

Frank wants us all to get to the point, and in thirty seconds, since there are time constraints in business, today more than ever before, and there are also attention span concerns as well.

Chapter Two

⬢ ⬢ ⬢

Typical Negative and Positive
Characters at Work and How to
Understand and Handle Each One

Strategy #6
Dealing With Negative Personality Types

W*e all encounter negative* personality types at the workplace. By figuring out which type you are dealing with, you will have a better chance at not taking his or her behavior personally. We will focus, first, on the top harmful types who may try to derail your career (the positive types are discussed in Strategy #7) because nearly all of us need help in better understanding and coping with these.

THE VAMPIRE

Vampires may be a pop culture phenomenon in literature and film, but they aren't a fun type to encounter at work even though, sadly, they do exist. Far from lurking in shadows, these workplace vampires walk among us, and they can be quite friendly until—just like the vampire who drains the blood of another creature in order to survive—they feed off of their co-workers by victimizing them to advance the vampire's own career. These vampires, whether male or female, coworker or boss, are adept at making themselves look good by making everyone else look bad. They drain your energy and enthusiasm by ordering you around and piling on the work. To make things worse, they also can feed on your insecurities so that you begin to feel less competent (even when performing tasks that were supposed to be the vampire's job in the first place).

When the vampire is the boss, the situation is compounded because he often doesn't provide the direction you need to do your job as efficiently and seamlessly as possible. This type knows what they *don't* want, but they can rarely articulate what they *do* want. So it's back and forth between you and this vampire until you either get it right, or you throw your hands up in exasperation, which can put your own career or reputation at risk. Usually it's better to try to win over the vampire instead of risk being seen as a poor team player or, in today's tough job market, to quit without another job to go to.

WHAT MAKES THE VAMPIRE TICK?

What might cause someone to be a vampire at work? Hate, guilt, and love, according to psychoanalyst Ernest Jones, are some of the repressed emotions behind the mythological vampire's blood-sucking actions. The workplace vampire has very mixed feelings about work and coworkers. He (or she) feels anger that his achievements are less than stellar; guilty about his unfulfilled career expectations; and hatred toward those who may have more talent and enthusiasm. There may even be an unconscious desire to love the very worker that is being victimized! This is what is known in psychology as a reaction formation: the vampire actually desires the person whose life blood is sucked, but, since he feels it is impossible to act on that desire, he behaves in a hostile manner, feeding off the victim.

When Brenda was 28, she was hired as a publicity assistant at a communications company in White Plains, New York. For the first few years, things went well for Brenda. But, gradually, Brenda became aware that her boss, Natalie, whom Brenda described as a vampire boss, had developed a pattern of fixating on a certain employee that she then systematically brought to his or her knees.

"As she moved up the ladder, Natalie basically became bitchier and bitchier," says Brenda.

Brenda wondered when it would be her turn. Her downfall at the company began when Natalie suddenly demoted Brenda's position from director to manager. Because of that demotion, Brenda's reserved parking space was taken away. At meetings, Natalie would refer to Brenda as a JAP, short for "Jewish American Princess," a totally inappropriate way of referring to someone in any situation, let alone a work setting.

Natalie grew increasingly critical and negative about Brenda's work. She was definitely trying to drive Brenda out, but Brenda wanted to be the one to triumph. Since she intended to start a family anyway, Brenda found that Natalie's negative behavior motivated her to shorten her timetable as the way to deal with her vampire boss: "Natalie was not going to be able to do a damn thing about it. I had made sure I made my announcement about my pregnancy before she got me out," Brenda says.

Not only did Brenda get her three month paid maternity leave, but soon after returning to work, with the environment still negative and hostile, Brenda broke her toe. That led to several additional months of paid disability leave. By the time Brenda turned in her resignation, she had had eight months of paid leave.

I asked Brenda why she had not gone to human resources with her complaints about Natalie. She explained that human resources reported to Natalie, so that would not have been an effective recourse. She did once try going over Natalie's head, to the head of the company, who told Brenda that she had to "work it out" with Natalie directly.

HOW TO DEAL WITH THE VAMPIRE
BEFORE YOUR BLOOD IS SUCKED DRY

What do you do if you are dealing with workplace vampires

and you do not want to, or cannot, leave? Can you try to turn the situation around?

It is obviously a challenging situation because if you overreact and let the vampire boss know that they're getting to you, they often will become even more ruthless. Unfortunately you cannot ignore the situation because the vampire will continue to consume your life blood until you are completely drained—leaving you professionally and emotionally dead.

You need to proactively attempt to turn the situation around in one of two ways. The first way is to embrace their nastiness, as hard as that may seem at first. Have you heard the expressions, "kill them with kindness," or "you can catch more bees with honey than with vinegar"? That is one way to deal with the vampire. Be kind. Be gracious. Do not let them feel that their blood-sucking ways repel you or that will just make them more brutal and nasty.

The second approach is to start to suck *their* blood so that you are the victor and not the victim. This of course can be very difficult for you to do since those who are victimized by the vampire tend to be sweet, caring, and positive people. You must let it be known that you can be an aggressor as well and that you will stand tall rather than buckle to the vampire's will. (Brenda, by taking her maternity leave and then, because of her unfortunate fall, additional disability leave, sees herself as having made the company, and her vampire boss, "pay" so that Brenda, who still feels anger and annoyance at how her ex-boss treated her, felt like she was the victorious one.)

But beware of this role reversal: do not become enamored with the vampire persona or, unwittingly, you may find yourself falling permanently into that role. Use it only in this instance to be victorious over your vampire coworker or superior. Once you have achieved or regained the power at work or in the business relationship, allow yourself to be the kind, caring, and nurturing soul you truly are—at least till the next vampire that you have to deal with steps out of the shadows!

A third way of dealing with the workplace vampire if you cannot yet leave this job is to document in a very detailed way what you have and are accomplishing. This will be useful when you are job hunting and you need to dispel the unjustified myth of the vampire that you did not accomplish anything or enough at your job. If you have a detailed record of your achievements, that record will speak for itself helping to drown out the negative voice of the vampire who, unfortunately, cannot be pleased and also has unrealistic expectations about what could or should be achieved in a reasonable period of time.

THE STAR

If bells jingled and whistles blew as The Star entered through the revolving doors at the office building each morning, that would be just fine with this personality type. She (or he) needs to be in the limelight, and for him or her, there is no such thing as too much focus or attention.

Some people strive to become The Star and others have that distinction thrust upon them. For those uncomfortable in the limelight, "Stardom" could be an unpleasant experience. Either way, The Star is not as enviable a role as it might seem at first glance. A lot of people want to dethrone them, and may even glean a feeling of gratification from seeing the mighty fall. Rick Brenner of Chaco Canyon Consulting pointed out the Japanese proverb, *Deru kui wa utareru* ("The stake that sticks out gets hammered down.")

If you are "paying homage" to the role of The Star, remember that you may be undermining your team by putting undue emphasis on the achievements of one without stressing the triumphs of others.

The Star may have grown up in a home where there were several children and he had to compete to get attention. Or, she may have been an only child who accompanied her parents to social activities in which the adults made a huge fuss about what she was achieving, developing a strong need for her to stand out to get attention.

Ben was The Star at his last job and it was a very uncomfortable feeling for him. His supervisor kept telling everyone that he was the "best" that she ever worked with. As Ben explains: "For one thing, it made me feel isolated. Everyone else was pissed off at me, and when someone above me wasn't considered The Star, I felt like they wanted to kill me. You can only be The Star if you're the boss."

In time, Ben was fired and he thinks having been labeled The Star had at least something to do with it.

If you want to avoid getting fired because you are considered The Star, here is what you should do: remember that only the boss can be The Star. It goes under the harsh reality that if you do "too good" a job, especially in a workplace/team situation, it can sometimes hurt you. You don't want to make your boss look bad. Continue to be the supporting player and you'll survive. If you have others at your same level with whom you work, and with whom you are compared, you want to avoid always being singled out as The Star. If you are a reluctant star, like Ben, try these tactics:

- Be discreet about any praise you receive and how you share any accolades. There is a fine line between receiving attention and being the object of scorn.
- Even if others label you The Star, you still can avoid acting like a *prime Dona* or a VIP who may cause others to be jealous or envious in a competitive and vicious way.
- By contrast, if you find yourself coping with the Star who loves being a Star, here are some suggested strategies:
- Remind The Star that she is putting herself in a position that might backfire in the long run.

- Remember that someone can still be admired and respected without being The Star.
- Help The Star to value his own personality traits rather than only his career achievements so his need to be the center of attention at work may eventually diminish.

THE CONTROL FREAK

Always having the first (and last) word, needing to be the one to make all the decisions—these are the hallmarks of The Control Freak. This person feels she has to make every decision related to your activities, from where you're going for lunch, to having the last word in the press release that you're crafting— even if it already was just fine.

George worked for Dan, a CEO who was a Control Freak. Dan had to be the master of everything, with everyone in the department falling in line with Dan's timetable. "He was a micromanager," says George. "It made me feel incompetent and out of control. My life wasn't my own. Dan expected me to be on call seven days a week, twenty-four hours a day. Everything had to be done his way—even if it was the wrong way, it had to be *his* way."

What makes someone a Control Freak? This trait usually appears within someone who feels he has little control in other areas of his life. It's a cliché but it is often true: the Control Freak at work is dramatically different at home, where her husband may boss her around, or his children seem to tell their father what to do, whereas at the workplace, the Control Freak feels like the king of his castle. Or, there may be childhood roots whereby his parents were authoritarian and that is the only leadership style that the Control Freak was exposed to growing up. Now in a position of authority at work, those old patterns kick-in; he may be unaware of how dominating and controlling his behavior is to others, who deserve to be treated with greater respect and courtesy.

How do you deal with The Control Freak? Of course, as with all these types, you have to take into account what position The Control Freak occupies at the company or in your career. Is she the boss? A coworker? An employee? A client? Customer? Service provider? If you are coworkers and at the same level, there is less justification for The Control Freak to tell you what to do than if he is your boss. Since it was George's boss who was The Control Freak, he had to tread lightly in how he dealt with this type. "I tried not to let it get me down," says George. "I tried to accept that that's the way he was and work around it. I kept doing the best job I could knowing that no matter what I did, it wasn't going to be good enough. But I needed the job. I couldn't tell him to go—himself."

Here are some additional suggestions for dealing with The Control Freak:

- If you are coworkers, try to let him or her take control over some of the mundane and insignificant details related to a situation or project so that the bigger issues can be handled by you without as much resistance.
- Try to divide decisions and to even-up the work load, with each person having responsibility for her own tasks or projects. That can help The Control Freak to have only so much control.
- If it is your boss who acts this way, remind yourself that he is probably just playing a role and it has little to do with you. Humor him by letting him play The Control Freak part because you know it's only a game.
- Admit that you also have high standards, but there has to be a way to agree that all standards can be met and are attainable. Try to pin this type down to concrete goals and specifications so that reaching those milestones is easier to document.

- If the Control Freak type does express positive feedback, even if it is only now and then, make sure you reinforce that reaction rather than the negative ones. Be appreciative of their rare appreciation!
- Try teaming up The Control Freak with someone who is easier to please so they have to reach a consensus.
- Remember that the excessive demands are a reflection of this person's personality trait rather than a statement about your competence. Do not take their criticism of you or your work personally.
- On the other hand, do you recognize yourself in this type? If you do, work on overcoming it so you become known as someone with high standards rather than someone who is a control freak who is also overly demanding. Avoid manifesting this trait; it will stand in the way of your getting a reputation as a first-rate manager or someone who is good to work with.

THE "IT'S NOT MY FAULT" BLAMELESS TYPE

Everyone makes mistakes, but the "It's Not My Fault" Blameless type would have you believe that it's *never* his fault. The fact that he truly miscalculates, uses poor judgment, or commits a faux pas is completely beside the point. Why is this attitude so detrimental in the workplace or in business? Whether it is a coworker, boss, employee, service provider, or business associate, this type not only denies responsibility but often tries to pin the blame on someone else—including you.

What causes this behavior? Think back to the formative years. Were you raised by parents who made you feel that no matter what you said and did, it was telling the truth that counted? Or was there a fear of admitting wrongdoing—a fear so strong that lying and denying blame, or even putting the blame, wrongly, on someone else seemed the better option? In the business world, someone with this trait tends to be a grownup version of the childhood adage, "Who stole the cookie from the cookie jar?" with fingers always pointing away.

If that was the childhood pattern, and if the "It's Not My Fault" Blameless Type does not have an epiphany, then this behavior is bound to continue. Learning from the example of others to admit wrongdoing, and to learn from your mistakes are both positive steps toward reversing this childhood pattern.

Claire had this orientation at work. If her manager pointed out that she had not gotten to a priority request, instead of saying, "Yes, thanks for the reminder, and I've put it on my priority 'to do' list for next week," her knee-jerk response would be to say something defensive like, "I wasn't asked to do that!" Sometimes it turned out that there actually was a miscommunication between Claire and her manager, but it took longer to figure that out because of her initial denial of responsibility. In time, Claire learned that if she simply accepted that she had failed to do something, or misunderstood what her work load was supposed to be, then she and her manager could figure out a way to streamline their interactions, with Claire's productivity improving a great deal.

If you detect that you're dealing with The Blameless type, try these strategies:

- Document, document, document. Keep excellent records detailing your efforts so you can defend yourself if you are (falsely) accused of being responsible for the mistakes that were really caused by the "It's Not My Fault" Blameless type.
- Try to be empathetic. He or she probably had overly critical parents so try to help minimize those critical voices by reassuring him or her with, "Look, we all make mistakes," and reminding him or her that making occasional mistakes is normal.

- If the "It's Not My Fault" Blameless type does manage to own up to an error, do not overreact or overemphasize the situation else they might retreat from such an admission in the future.

If you are the one with this personality type, apply the above suggestions to yourself. Remind yourself, whether you are an employee or the boss, that no one, including you, is perfect and that admitting a mistake will humanize you to your employees.

Most of all, you can set an example that admitting a mistake is okay. That way, someone who has this trait will see that he might at least open up to the possibility that there are those who do take responsibility for their decisions and that being wrong once in a while is not the end of the world.

Placing the blame on others rarely works in business especially if you are the person in charge. Even if your subordinate is the one who goofs, the questions still fall back onto you (e.g., "Why did you let that happen? Why didn't you see this coming?"). Even if it is your subordinate's fault, you have to solve the problem since you are stuck with the consequences.

It's not just speaking the words, "I messed up," that counts, especially if it is a boss taking responsibility for the actions of subordinates that led to a less than favorable outcome, but really trying to understand what happened and how things could go differently, and better, next time.

USA Today columnist Craig Wilson took a whimsical approach to the issue of taking responsibility for one's mistakes in his column on the topic, "Mistakes are like passwords: We all make 'em." The column was inspired by Pulitzer Prize-winning journalist Joseph Hallinan's book, *Why We Make Mistakes: How We Look without Seeing, Forget Things in Seconds, and Are all Pretty Sure We are Way above Average.*

Or, as the great English idiom puts it, "To err is human, to forgive divine."

THE SABOTEUR

Beware The Saboteur! This is the coworker, partner, employee, or service provider who is willing to betray you big time. Steve, who took Bill's assistant and a lot of his business away to start a rival company, is an example of The Saboteur. Another example is that of someone who is a real disrupter at work. As a coworker of a Saboteur explains: "If he thinks I'm on deadline or I need to work without distraction, he always provides a distraction, almost like he wants me *not* to succeed." The Saboteur's conscious or unconscious wish to see someone else fail is not that uncommon.

At the weekly staff meeting, Claudia volunteered the services of Gordon, a coworker, because another coworker, Jake, led her to believe that Gordon had said "yes" to Claudia's request. There was a brief awkward moment when Claudia realized her error; she apologized for the confusion, excused Gordon from the commitment, and thought that was the end of it.

A week later, however, Gordon shared with the staff an important e-mail requesting everyone provide feedback by the next day on a new product that was crucial to the company. Everyone except Claudia got that e-mail. Coincidence? Or the act of an unwitting Saboteur?

Dealing with The Saboteur calls for some or all of these strategies:

- "Know thy enemy." Be aware of this individual and what he is up to.
- Do not let your guard down around The Saboteur.
- Be wary of using humor or sarcasm in front of The Saboteur. If she lacks a sense of humor, she could take your comments as genuine, with The Saboteur even reporting you to a superior for what you said in jest.

- When someone is The Saboteur, try to analyze and scrutinize your current and previous interactions. If you think there could be a misunderstanding behind The Saboteur's action, trying to straighten it out before things escalate. That is what Claudia did. She apologized again to Gordon, who of course said he was not upset about what happened, even though Claudia knew that he was; but, he did not try to undermine her, or act like The Saboteur, again.

If you recognize yourself as The Saboteur, work hard on understanding why you act that way and how you can achieve the same goals without being devious and oppositional.

THE IDEA THIEF

You may be wined and dined and think you're being treated like a best friend, but The Idea Thief is just biding his or her time, working to gain your trust so you'll spill the beans about your latest project, idea, or invention. As a 38-year-old woman who works for an educational company, explains: "The big company we all work for stole some of my program ideas and gave them to a competing travel company, and my colleagues did nothing about it. They could have complained on my behalf, but they chose not to. I lost money and influence within the company structures through their behavior."

Dealing with The Idea Thief can lead to a double betrayal: your ideas are stolen and no one does anything about it. Coworkers have to be careful about overtly or inadvertently taking credit for a colleague's ideas. There is a definite emphasis on being part of a team at most companies, but you still can keep your name associated with the parts of a project or the specific ideas that are yours. If you find your boss is The Idea Thief, this will be a more challenging situation. Your boss may see taking your ideas and presenting those concepts as his (or her) own as acceptable and even expected. (Remember the movie *Working Girl* from the 1980s? Melanie Griffith's boss, played by Sigourney Weaver, tried to pass off her secretary's ideas as her own. The boss was clearly portrayed as a villain for trying to do that.)

Very secure bosses will usually give credit where credit is due whether the idea is from a high level executive or an unpaid intern.

Some ways to deal with The Idea Thief include:

- Be self-protective by copyrighting or patenting your ideas before you show anything to The Idea Thief.
- You may even want to keep your ideas to yourself.
- If you work for a company and it is part of your job to generate ideas—and the company will own whatever ideas you develop—you will still want to avoid others stealing your ideas. Getting credit for your original concepts may mean the difference between a promotion and an increase in pay and more status, or being seen as an underperformer who might even be let go.
- If you know that someone is The Idea Thief, see if you can try to build up his confidence in his own contributions so he will not need to steal ideas from others. Praise his efforts so he won't feel as much resentment about his co-workers' ideas and accomplishments. (The Idea Thief, after all, usually does not see herself as capable of generating any original ideas that others would want to grab.)
- If you see yourself as an occasional or habitual Idea Thief, work on building up your own self-esteem so you do not have to steal others' innovations.
- If you know you have lots of original ideas, and you find yourself interacting with someone who shares a similar

thought, let that person know that you independently came up with a similar idea.

THE ENTITLED

According to The Entitled, the world owes him everything, making it especially hard for everyone who works for him or with him. Some see The Entitled as a generational issue with those born during a certain time period more likely to be in The Entitled category. Others see it as a personality type. Whether you work with The Entitled, or you realize you sometimes act that way yourself, this trait rarely serves anyone well in the workplace or in business.

Belinda was a recent college graduate of twenty-one in an entry-level position who resented her salary and that her job combined clerical or administrative chores (like using the photocopy machine) with the more creative ones. She needed to learn how to prioritize her workload; in the meantime, she would rather leave numerous key tasks undone than work extra hours to get caught up. Rather than discuss her disillusionment with her boss, she quit and took another job, with a shorter commute, leaving her boss high and dry, and then asked for a recommendation.

It can actually help The Entitled to start out in the workplace in an entry-level position so she can work her way up. Doing chores and tasks that seem menial or beneath them may help this type become a bit more humble. Too often, however, if The Entitled is the offspring of those who also see themselves as entitled this next generation may have been helped or encouraged to skip some steps. They may see starting at a job on the second or third rung of the ladder, rather than at the bottom, as the path that they intrinsically deserve.

Meet the challenge of dealing with The Entitled by:

- Letting The Entitled know what the expectations are for everyone with no exceptions.
- Avoid the temptation of giving The Entitled menial or meaningless work just to teach them a lesson. This can backfire and reinforce their disdain for less challenging work. Help them see the lesson in these tasks.
- Take heart in the reality that this is a phase that new hires will eventually get over (or they could be out of a job before long.)

If you recognize The Entitled in yourself, vow to avoid acting like you have anything coming to you whether this is your first or your tenth job. If you have accepted a job or project, be humble and agree to perform whatever task a specific job requires—whatever your age or your skill level.

THE LIAR

This is not the person who uses white lies to be tactful or polite. No, The Liar is a pathological liar who cannot help bending the truth to look better or to try to sink someone else's achievements. Whether it's inflated sales figures that are complete lies or fabricated stories that put him (or her) in a better light, The Liar has a problem that is not going to be cured overnight.

Catching The Liar in a lie, and discussing, between the two of you, what happened and how it could be very embarrassing or possibly entail legal ramifications if the lie were brought to the attention of the authorities might put enough fear into The Liar that she will mend her ways. Provide an example of consistency within your own integrity and honesty so that you are setting the tone and the model against which others will see themselves. It may sound petty, but even lying about something as innocuous as one's age can unwittingly justify lying for convenience and send the unspoken message that lying is tolerated in the workplace.

Help The Liar understand that if they are asked questions that have little to do with business or are inappropriate in a work context, such as your marital status or your salary, a simple, "I prefer not to answer that question," is a better response than lying. As Julie Jansen, author of *You Want Me to Work With Whom?* said when interviewed: "Unfortunately I think people who are very skilled liars become very good at controlling their body language. Me, for example, I'm a terrible liar. I fidget or have shifty eye contact. People who are skilled liars—you can't figure it out because they have themselves convinced."

Here are some of the additional ways that Carol Kinsey Goman, author of *The Nonverbal Advantage*, lists to help you determine if someone is being deceptive: "Incongruence between what's being said and the speaker's body language (like saying 'no' while nodding 'yes'); an increased blink rate—especially over 50 blinks per minutes—or eyelid flutter; gazing downward after asserting innocence; shorter, less descriptive statements; dilated pupils; and face touching—especially around the mouth and nose."

If you are dealing with The Liar, try to:

- Protect yourself by being very clear about the facts and truths at all times.
- Avoid accusing someone of being a "liar" unless absolutely necessary since name-calling is not going to reflect well on you.
- Document your work and your achievements so that "your side of the street" always can be shown to be in good order, even if someone else around you is caught in a web of lies.

THE GOSSIP

Share confidential or private information with The Gossip at your peril since it will probably be repeated to other coworkers or even to your boss whether or not such sharing is in your best interest. The Gossip can ruin someone's reputation very quickly as rumors spread like wildfire! This can cause a panic at the company if the gossip is about job losses or company troubles, planting suspicion and insecurity when confidence and positive attitudes serve everyone better.

What causes someone to be The Gossip? There could be a need to be liked or accepted. If The Gossip is perceived to have "inside" information on someone, including the company, they may perceive that they could be allowed into inner circles or cliques of coworkers or friends who might otherwise exclude her (or him). There is also The Gossip who does it to gain the upper hand at work and The Gossip who does it because she thinks it humanizes the workplace by sharing information about coworkers or the boss that goes beyond work boundaries. The Gossip who is doing it to create a more cohesive workplace probably doesn't see his tendency to share bits of personal or confidential information as being malicious or an undesirable trait but instead, considers himself to be simply passing along information, or is sharing the latest news as a way to bond with others.

Sandra was The Gossip at her office, sharing information about certain coworkers that could give other coworkers, those with whom she felt a bond, and upper hand in their competitive work environment. With half a dozen coworkers competing for just one promotion to the next rung on the ladder, Sandra, who was in an administrative capacity, saw it as her job to befriend each coworker so she could find out as much information as possible that she could then pass along to that coworker's competitors. Once an employee figured out what Sandra was up to, they would withhold any personal or professional information that might be misused by Sandra. But until an employee figured out Sandra's role as The Gossip at work, it could be too late to stop the spread of rumors that were accepted as fact by coworkers and supervisors and undermined that employee's goals.

For example, Sandra set up one of the employees with an interview with a friend of hers who had a consulting company. When the employee went on the interview, at Sandra's suggestion, Sandra then used that situation as proof that the employee was actively seeking additional work as a consultant and was not totally committed to her current job. The fact that Sandra had suggested the interview, or that many of the employees had outside consulting jobs, was never mentioned. Months later, when the coworker was up for review, it was brought up in her assessment that she had been actively seeking out other job opportunities and was not completely committed to her job—even though Sandra had set her up and then gossiped to everyone about the employee's private career matters.

If you are dealing with The Gossip, here are some strategies that might be helpful to you:

- Let him or her know that you won't listen to badmouthing of colleagues, bosses, or even sharing unsubstantiated company rumors. If The Gossip starts to tell you something that you don't want to hear, do something dramatic, like cover your ears and say, "I'm just not listening to these rumors and innuendos" and walk away.

- Once you know that someone is The Gossip, whether it is out of maliciousness or neediness, deliberating withhold any personal or professional information that could be shared behind your back.

You should also scrutinize your own behavior. Rumors about pregnancies, romantic attachments or detachments, upcoming trips or excursions, family behavioral issues or challenges, career aspirations or job inquiries, all are areas that can be ripe for sharing but also can cast you in the role of The Gossip—no matter how friendly and harmless your intentions may be. If you stop the trait in yourself, you might set a standard for your department, or your colleagues, that others will be more likely to replicate.

THE INCOMPETENT

Unlike The Shirker (described later on), who has the ability but just does not exercise it, The Incompetent simply doesn't possess the skills, intelligence or personality for their job. It could be a disconnect between the individual and the requirements of the position, or it could be a deep-seated incompetence due to inconsistent or poor training, or having someone completely unprepared or in the wrong position.

Susan was thrilled to get a job as an administrative assistant with a multiplicity of job responsibilities, from writing correspondence to answering the phone to making "cold calls" or sales calls. The only problem: Susan did not like to use the phone. She did not see herself as a "phone person." Alas, that was at least fifty percent of the requirements of her job and without that key element to her job responsibilities, not only did the company risk a loss in the growth in revenue that those calls, done effectively, could bring in but Susan was not going to get a positive recommendation from her supervisor. In this case, Susan's incompetence was caused by her personality, which was very shy, but, more importantly, by her reluctance to get training and help that could move her beyond those limitations caused by her personality preferences. Within a few months, Susan realized that this type of all-purpose job was not working out for her and she quit that job. When she looked for a new job, she went out of her way to make sure that the job lacked any sales functions including cold calling or soliciting business through e-mail or in person.

In some jobs, having to deal with The Incompetent can mean that you have to do your work and theirs, until he or she is replaced or voluntarily leaves out of their own frustration and embarrassment. But in other jobs, such as the health care industry or law enforcement, having to deal with The Incompetent could be putting your life or the lives of others in jeopardy. You need to make a very careful judgment call about when it is your moral duty to go to a supervisor, manager, boss, human resources director, even a professional association review board and report that a coworker is putting the lives of others at risk.

If you recognize that some of your skills are rusty and need upgrading, or that you need some knowledge that you are lacking, be proactive and take courses, seek out mentors or teachers, start reading more, or take continuing education courses to acquire or keep up with the skills that are necessary to do your job well. Check with human resources. Your company might have a policy of paying some or all of the cost of professional education courses or tuition for acquiring an undergraduate or graduate degree to improve your competence.

THE MANIPULATOR

When you deal with The Manipulator, you walk out of a meeting smiling, until you suddenly realize that you've been talked into taking on more projects than you can possibly handle. But The Manipulator told you how talented and efficient you are. You were initially flattered and now you feel manipulated. If you try to back down from these requests, you could be labeled The Shirker.

What makes someone The Manipulator? A lifetime of being unable to deal directly with people about his (or her) needs. The Manipulator relies on trickery or deceit to force people to do what he needs and wants through indirect coercion, cajoling, or even holding threats or material gains over their heads. The typical manipulator is unaware of what he is doing. This approach to getting what he wants is so ingrained in him that it is just the way he connects and interacts with others. Somewhere in his past, a parent, a teacher, or someone else close to The Manipulator behaved in this manner; the trait has been passed along from generation to generation, just like hair color or blood type. Without becoming aware of this tendency and making a concerted effort to change his ways by being straight on and dealing directly with people, The Manipulator will go through work or personal situations using these sneaky methods again and again.

Bill wants his employees to be the best they can be but rather than have a weekly meeting in which he repeats that rallying cry, he sets up competitive situations between employees and outside consultants so they are manipulated into performing out of fear that they will be perceived in a lesser light than the rival set up by their boss. Who is copied on e-mails, and even when or why e-mails are responded to, is handled in an inconsistent way; inconsistency is a trait of The Manipulator. Whereas most work environments thrive on known and consistent goals and procedures, The Manipulator, because of his own background, recreates in his workplace the inconsistencies he knew in his formative years.

If you are dealing with The Manipulator, here are some helpful strategies:

- Be aware that you are dealing with The Manipulator so you are less likely to be suckered in the first place. Since inconsistency is part of this type's behavior, you will have to stick to your decision that you are dealing with this type even when he (or she) temporarily reverts to acting in a normal, consistent, and non-manipulative way.
- If you are manipulated by this person and you take on more work than you can possibly handle, or more than you should be dealing with in the first place, you can try

to find someone to assist you so the work will get done and you are not backing down.

- Rehearse your answers so you will be ready next time if this type asks you to volunteer, or to take on additional responsibilities that are outside of your agreed upon job description. The Manipulator usually has the uncanny ability to know your weaknesses to be accepted and approved of and to play to them, so stand strong when you deal with this type.

THE BROWN NOSER

As a certain financial services executive used to say, "I may be brown, but I'm still around." So why is The Brown Noser the object of so much scorn? Or, if you are one, why do others seem to dislike you? The Brown Noser takes a trait that most everyone shares in business, wanting to succeed and wanting the boss to like you, and kicks it up too many notches so that it's not genuine and is obvious to everyone.

The Brown Noser acts this way because it worked for him (or her) throughout his early years. (Think of the Eddie Haskell character on the old "Leave It To Beaver" television show.) Or, he (or she) may have grown up in a family of several siblings, and the way to get attention was to be the one who always did what was asked. During the school years, this person might have gotten an A partly because she was always making an effort to be known personally by the teacher and praising the teacher for her efforts so that the teacher was even unaware that this student's brown nosing ways were having a positive impact on her grade.

Of course this is a trait that you can ignore. It's certainly not as insidious or disruptive as the bully (see Strategy #47 – Handle the Workplace Bully - for help with bullies at work). But it can still be very annoying. Everyone else, including you, is working hard and doing what needs to be done, but the Brown Noser, because he is always praising the boss, or waxing eloquently about the wonderful work of a coworker, is getting kudos and even raises that seem disproportionate to what he is really accomplishing on the job.

You could mirror the behavior of The Brown Noser but, if doing so is just not in your nature, this technique could backfire. If you come across as strained and forced, and too obvious, then *you* might be labeled The Brown Noser—whereas, someone who truly acts this way has perfected this approach to the extent that his ingratiating ways go unnoticed by most others, especially the one that he is aiming to please.

When dealing with The Brown Noser:

- Remember they have a very strong need to please authority figures. Do not stand in their way of trying to get that praise, but don't be cast aside or put down, yourself, because of it.
- Try not to make fun of The Brown Noser even though her need to please is so obvious and obnoxious.
- Do not let The Brown Noser take away your own legitimate chances of shining in the authority figure's eyes.

If you are a Brown Noser and you feel that others are resenting you for it, you may just have to work on your technique a bit more so your efforts to win over management are not so obvious.

THE BOASTER

Everyone tends to boast just a little but The Boaster does it too often and in a way that makes those around him (or her) feel diminished and resentful. Practically everyone has encountered The Boaster although you may have known him or her by a different name: The Braggart.

How do you handle this personality type? Perhaps you really want to work with this person because they are knowledgeable and have something to share, but being around The Boaster goes against your grain. (You may have competition issues in the workplace that are not helping you, but that is one of your own background traits that you need to deal with.)

When someone stops by to discuss the business at hand, The Boaster might say something like, "I have a $500,000 team meeting waiting for me at one o'clock and I'm so excruciatingly busy. I really work better with appointments. Can we make an appointment to talk?" Someone who is not The Boaster might rephrase that, and get a better outcome by saying, "I am rushing to a one o'clock team meeting and since I know you're also very busy, could we set up another appointment that is mutually convenient?"

The Boaster may have always heard his (or her) parents brag about him. Or quite the opposite might be true: her parents withheld praise so much that she has an excessive need for it. At school, or in previous jobs, The Boaster may have seen others, or himself, singled out for achievements, and it created the need to keep repeating that type of attention for his accomplishments. Feeling good inside about her achievements at work is not enough; she has internalized a need for others, especially those in positions of authority, to praise her.

At weekly staff meetings, Sophie found herself sharing so many of her accomplishments during that week with her boss and coworkers that the meeting dragged on fifteen minutes longer than originally planned. Were her coworkers accomplishing a lot less than Sophie, or was she insistent on boasting about each and everything so she was perceived as "the best"? Sophie realized she had to rein-in her need to boast so that the meeting would go faster. The next time, she just highlighted one or two items of greatest interest rather than saturating the room with too many details.

Do not avoid the Boaster all together. You can still benefit by following through with this person, even though the trait has turned you off. Why? You get to work on any competition issues or insecurities you might have and discover why dealing with The Boaster is so offensive to you. You also demonstrate to yourself that you are bigger than your emotions and that business is business. Finally, maybe there are positive traits beyond The Boaster's rough exterior that you will uncover if you give this person another chance.

On the other hand, try these strategies to deal with this trait if you recognize it within yourself:

- Instead of being The Boaster who causes envy, jealousy, and resentment, finds others to do the boasting for you.
- If you are in a creative business, hire a manager or an agent to be The Boaster for you.
- If you lack an agent or manager, and you have to sell yourself to others, err on the side of underplaying your achievements without being so modest that you fail to make a strong, favorable impression.
- Become secure in yourself and what you've accomplished without feeling you have to share it with everyone before it "really" matters.

THE SHIRKER

As long as you do not have to work for or with The Shirker, it is the company's, or someone else's problem. But if you and The Shirker are teamed together, or if you depend on each other for parts of a project so you can go forward, The Shirker can directly hold you back. He (or she) can make your life miserable at work or even threaten your job security.

Beau was The Shirker at his company. He would agree to do something for the two bosses that he reported to, but if he failed to finish that task, he would go on to another task rather than keep working until the job was done. Since two people were directly counting on him, being The Shirker had negative consequences for his supervisors as well as for the overall productivity of the company. Like many shirkers, Beau was inconsistent in how he approached his work load. He shirked some requests but fulfilled, and even excelled, at others. His inconsistency made it harder for those who managed him to justify taking certain tasks out of Beau's hands completely since he did, on occasion, finish what he started. If Beau wants to get a positive evaluation from his supervisors, and if he wants to cultivate a reputation as a go-getter and as someone who completes the tasks that he has been assigned, he needs to work on his reputation as well as his tendency to play the role of The Shirker.

What causes someone to be like this? In previous jobs, or even during the school years, there was an inconsistent standard set up that this individual adopted as his or her universal approach to responsibility. Perhaps when something fell through the cracks at home, at camp, or at school, it was glossed over. Being inconsistent became acceptable, or at least tolerated, so he (or she) did not learn the potentially grave consequences of being The Shirker, whether occasionally or all the time. Furthermore, this person might have had a parent who did something for him when he was The Shirker. For example, if, as a teenager, he was told, "Clean up your room," if his room was not clean, and a parent, or paid help, cleaned it up for him, he may consciously or unconsciously be expecting someone to come along at work and finish those tasks for him. In the workplace, or in business, someone else actually may come along and help him to get the work done, but word will get out that he is less productive than required, or that others are needed to bail him out of his work load. This is definitely not the way to advance one's career. Traits that were tolerated in childhood, the teen years, or even young adulthood, have to be addressed at work or in business if one is to succeed.

As with Beau, The Shirker may not be consistently shirking his duties. Try to see the pattern as to what he procrastinates on and puts aside. Who is asking The Shirker to do these tasks? Is it a coworker? Boss? Client? Customer? If you know of a time when The Shirker was consistently reliable, try to find out the circumstances of those triumphs and figure out how you could help The Shirker to duplicate those accomplishments.

If you are dealing with a Shirker:

- Rather than just criticizing The Shirker and making him feel even worse about himself, see if you can increase his motivation to get something done.
- Nagging will rarely work and even if it does, the bad feeling that nagging causes may create bigger problems in the long run than getting The Shirker to do a specific job.
- Make sure this is really your problem. Observing someone not doing his job as effectively as possible, when it doesn't impact you in any way, especially if this person does not report to you, isn't your issue. His lack of performance will be discovered in time.

THE DOOMSAYER

This type will gladly tell you why something won't work rather than how it could be beneficial. It can be debilitating and draining to work with The Doomsayer (aka The Downer). Everything you suggest, every plan you have, every fresh idea you pitch is the subject of criticism and doubt. "But…" is the favorite word of The Doomsayer. This person can find the negative in anything! They suck the life and energy out of a positive team.

The Doomsayer may have been raised in a home where there was a lot of sickness or financial disappointment. Every time she (or he) felt positive about things, someone's health took a turn for the worse, or a parent's job was lost, or salary cut drastically. As a result, she grew up feeling afraid—always waiting for the other shoe to fall.

If things are going well, she is fearful that something bad will come along to offset the positive. Like so many of these personality traits, The Doomsayer tendency is often passed on from parent to child; growing up in an atmosphere of negativity, it is challenging to develop a positive attitude. This personality type is pessimistic and fearful; she is also needy but, sadly, being The Doomsayer tends to push people away, increasing her neediness, so a vicious cycle is set up.

If things are going well at work, you can always count on Patricia to throw in something negative and pessimistic. It would be helpful if she was pointing out some business trends or industry developments that should be watched and noted, but Patricia is The Doomsayer who has to throw cold water on everything no matter what. It is her nature. If someone is going on vacation to a nice sunny location, she can't help but say, "I hope it doesn't rain every day." If someone shares positive sales figures for the week, she has to say, "Is that going to use up our inventory faster than we can replace it?" It has gotten to the point where no one wants to talk to Patricia because they know she will throw cold water on anything positive that they share or introduce a negative thought to everything that is going on at the company or in their lives. As a result, Patricia is far more isolated than she should be, which makes her feel sadder and more negative, which leads to her being even more of The Doomsayer.

If you have to cope with The Doomsayer, try some of these tactics:

- As with so many of those who evidence these negative traits, you have to remind yourself that The Doomsayer's viewpoint is just that and not necessarily reflective of reality.

- You can try to humor The Doomsayer: "Are you afraid if you like what I suggest people will accuse you of being too soft?" or "I know you're going to nix my suggestion but let me share it with you anyway."
- Try to maintain your positive attitude despite The Doomsayer's attempts to bring you down. You are responsible for your own mental state.
- Avoid associating with them in your down time. Hang out with coworkers who are positive and enthusiastic!

Strategy #7
Form Relationships With Positive Types

When you are lucky enough to find one or more of these positive types at your workplace, do not hesitate to befriend them and to form relationships. These are the people who will help you to thrive at work.

At the same time, it is vital that you see beyond the obvious label of "mentor" or "nurturer" and that you understand how those traits might backfire in your current or overall company or career growth if you do not keep your eyes open.

THE TRUSTWORTHY

This is one of the most pivotal traits in a fellow coworker that will help you to feel more comfortable and confident in the workplace and in business. The Trustworthy is someone who is consistent in his or her behavior and who makes good on commitments. Ask someone what trait they would most like in a coworker or boss and the response will often be someone who can be trusted.

Being The Trustworthy is an admirable trait in business and one that every single person in the business world should embrace. Those who are The Trustworthy, however, may hurt themselves if they naively assume that everyone else operates on that same principle of trust. Without testing someone out, and making sure someone earns his or her trust, The Trustworthy might inadvertently put the company or himself or herself in jeopardy.

THE MENTOR

The Mentor puts your growth and advancement as a primary concern. A genuine mentor will not be threatened by the strides that the mentee makes but will instead rejoice in his or her professional development. Although you and The Mentor may initially find it hard to be friends, since friendship might interfere with the mentoring role, a friendship might ensue from working so closely together. I have written about Nancy Creshkoff, my first boss at Macmillan Publishing Company, and I have described her as The Mentor. Succinctly, Nancy took her role of helping her employees to be the best they could be very seriously. Not only did she have weekly grammar classes that we attended, along with books that we had to buy and study, but she organized regular lunchtime or after work get-togethers at restaurants or at her home. Since Nancy was my first boss in publishing, she set a very high standard that I kept with me throughout the other fulltime or freelance jobs that I have had over the years. You know The Mentor when you have one. If you do not have one, try to seek one out at your job or, if that is not possible, through associations who set up mentorship programs. One program that comes to mind is Mystery Writers of America, which pairs accomplished pros with entry-level writers, as well as the Women's Media Group, which has a formal summer mentoring program for minority women who are accepted into their formal mentoring program in publishing and the media.

THE PARTNER

Rather than seeing you as a slave, if he or she is the boss, or as a threat, if you are coworkers, The Partner sees everyone at work as if you are in partnership together. All for one and one for all as the saying goes and it's a positive and very powerful approach to working together.

Ruth Perryman's former boss exemplified the role of The Partner. Ruth explains: "We were partners. It was a fundraising organization. He did all the fundraising and donor relations [and] I did all the budget stuff, HR stuff, and [we] left each other alone. Once a week, or more often as needed, we would clue each other in."

There are countless examples of The Partner who is perfect for that role and the partnership goes fine at work. But there are other examples where roles overlap too much, or there is too much competition, and the partnership starts to diminish in its value. If you find The Partner at work, it is key to reevaluate that partnership on a periodic basis. Not only do personalities change but situations change as well as market conditions that may dictate if the company needs to take management in a new direction. Those who partner may prefer to have only one person at the helm.

THE COACH/TRAINER

There are coworkers who just have to share with you everything they have learned. It is a great way to gain knowledge and insights without having to take a course or go for a training workshop. The Coach/Trainer gets a great deal of satisfaction from sharing his expertise with others. This can be extremely beneficial to the company especially if the information is something that the company needs and wants. But if The Coach/Trainer simply wants to share everything, from how to use new software no one else really cares about to the details of each of the course he or she attends at an annual retreat, the trait can be somewhat time-consuming and disruptive. The Coach/Trainer would do well to wait until asked by someone if he or she would share his or her expertise.

THE FACILITATOR

Helping others to share and guiding a discussion or even a department so it sets goal and has accountability about meeting those goals are traits of The Facilitator. The Facilitator can help to move discussions along; this is a role that is very much appreciated in small group situations. But if The Facilitator is performing this role in an informal capacity, it can set up some disputes over authority since performing this function usually sets this individual above the others as the director of the situation or discussion. Being The Facilitator can also set this person apart from others which, if team building and equality are goals for coworkers at a particular company, may render the formal or informal role of The Facilitator as someone who undermines the group's goals.

THE VISIONARY

When others are wondering what they are going to be doing for the weekend, or perhaps where to go on their next vacation, The Visionary is figuring out what the company should be doing in the next one, five, or ten years. The Visionary can be a wonderful asset to a department, company, or in an industry. Especially if The Visionary develops a track record of being correct in his or her visions, his or her opinion will be sought out.

If you know The Visionary, just be careful that you do not let his or her untested visions for the future either dictate what actions you will take or stop you from doing your own thinking and developing your own unique visions. If you are The Visionary, watch out that you are not so focused on the future that you are failing to put as much focus and energy into what you should be accomplishing on a daily or short-term basis.

There is an instinctive wisdom in The Visionary and it is not necessarily because of books read or degrees achieved. The Visionary is someone who can be an asset at work because he or she has an understanding about the goals of the company or the focus of a particular project. In business, The Visionary can help you to understand what is pivotal to doing well in your industry as well as what new trends need to be embraced or, conversely, ignored. Part of being the Visionary is what coach and workplace author Julie Jansen calls the key of self-awareness. Says Jansen: "If someone I work with always makes me communicate defensively, which nobody likes, I would realize that the minute they are going to open their mouth, I am going to repeat a mantra to myself [about keeping my cool no matter what]." Thus, by wisely remaining clued-in to the bigger picture, a negative confrontation is avoided.

THE MOTIVATOR

Unlike the nag, who makes you want to do the opposite because his or her nagging is so annoying, The Motivator has a knack for bringing out your best. He or she makes you feel proud and determined. The Motivator is the cheering squad for coworkers or management as well as for a product, company, or individual. Be mindful, though, about looking at the bigger picture; if The Motivator is just looking at what is positive and putting the emphasis on why something should be attempted there might not be the scrutiny of why it should be questioned and possibly shelved. Also, if someone else is The Motivator for you, you may become over-reliant on getting motivation from external sources rather than from within.

If you are The Motivator, you have to be careful that you are not putting so much time, energy, and motivation into the actions of your fellow coworkers or employees that you end up forgetting your own goals.

THE BELIEVER

"You can do it" is the Believer's philosophy. Why? Because you can! It's that simple. Others will have a list of reasons why you can't do it and maybe even a list of reasons why you can but The Believer has this gut; visceral feeling that you will do it and that's all there is to it. His or her belief in you is contagious in a very positive way. You need to be around The Believer when you're especially vulnerable because you're starting a new company, expressing a fresh idea, sharing a vision or a project that you are enthusiastic about. But since you're at the beginning of this thing, it may go either way—you can go forward, enthusiastic and determined, or you can shrink back and give up.

Buddy Hobart, the founder and head of Solutions 21, an organizational and strategic consulting firm based in Pittsburgh, shares about The Believer who was his first employee at his company, joining when the company was six months old. Says Hobart: "I was just beginning to formulate our vision for this place. She joined and she believed in the vision. We were sitting in the office and talking about how we will have people delivering programs around the world and we'll be in multiple locations and we'll have talent that will be in different parts of the country and different parts of the world all at the same time. She saw those possibilities when we literally had a one-room office. Her willingness to buy into that and to believe in that really motivated me to continue on the track and make it happen. That trust and faith and belief was an enormous motivator." Fourteen years later, The Believer is still with Hobart as his vice president of operations.

THE NEGOTIATOR

This is a handy person to have around if you know that your

workforce consists of individuals who tend to get into "head butting" situations. Of course there are professionals who negotiate as part of their job, but in this instance, we are addressing the personality trait of being a negotiator rather than someone who has to pick sides and have strong points of view that cannot be shifted. The Negotiator is able to intervene when it is necessary or, if it is between the Negotiator and just one other person, to compromise and find a middle ground. "Okay, you want to travel more but our budget's been cut so how about if you agree to travel a little less often and to be more mindful of your miscellaneous food and hotel bills when you do travel?"

THE PRAISER

Do you need a pat on the back? The Praiser is one to turn to. Scott Swanay, 44, who runs Fantasy Baseball Sherpa and Fantasy Football Sherpa, two website-based advisory services, had the good fortune to work for The Praiser when he was an actuary in the insurance business. He explains: "He and I worked very well together. He would acknowledge my efforts. When I did a good job on something, he would share that with other people. He would say something like, "We're really fortunate to have you. You're so diligent and good at what you do. I don't know what I'd do without you." He'd share it with other people via e-mail [and] that made me feel good. He made me feel motivated. He made me want to give an extra effort even though I didn't have a direct reporting [relationship to him]."

THE PROTECTOR

This type of person always has your back and that is especially important in business environments where you are not present all the time. The Protector is listening and looking out for you and, conversely, you are doing the same for others. If there are new rules or regulations that you should know about, The Protector clues you in. If you find out about something related to the job or work that will impact on you and others, you let everyone know.

The only downside of being The Protector is that you can be so focused on helping others and protecting them that you find yourself being left behind. It is therefore key to have enough self-interest that you are also serving as The Protector for yourself.

THE DEPENDABLE

This is a sought after, positive trait in business and one of the highest compliments you can pay to someone especially if he or she is in a job that requires that person to be what is known as a "self-starter." Part of being The Dependable is that you are also consistent and reliable.

The Dependable type generally needs to be wary of putting the need to be Dependable before being flexible when, for example, needing to get revised guidelines or deadlines because a project is taking longer than predicted, or circumstances have changed so additional time is actually beneficial. Being The Dependable "no matter what" can backfire; it is a terrific trait to have, overall, but it needs to be applied in each workplace or business situation. Here's another example when The Dependable can be at cross-purposes with coworkers: someone is so determined to show up at work, no matter what, that he or she drags himself into the office with a runny nose, or with a contagious illness that the whole department catches and is out sick within a day or two. Or out of fear of losing that label of the Dependable, someone refuses to take his or her legitimate vacation time, eventually burning out from exhaustion and information overload.

THE PEOPLE MAGNET

Everyone wants to be around The People Magnet. He or she has a way of gathering the best and the brightest around him or her whether it is in the company cafeteria at lunchtime or during the karaoke session on Friday night at the annual retreat for the association's chapter gathering. If you are The People Magnet, you will have an address book thick with friends, associates, and even people you have met on trains and planes with whom you stay in communication. This can be an especially great personality trait if you are in a business that requires a broad base of information so that all the people you are connected to serve to keep you in the loop with what's new in their fields or communities or even countries.

If you know The People Magnet, you know that he or she attracts people and that this can be a great trait for a sales person who needs to sell a product. If customers or clients want to be around a salesman, it can increase business.

The downside of being The People Magnet is that some with this trait don't know how or when to turn off being around people. They find it hard to allow themselves to have the quiet time that could help them to come up with more creative ideas for their companies or products. Or they are out socializing with people too much and not sitting back at the office doing the mundane but necessary paperwork that needs to be completed.

The People Magnet can also obscure the personalities of those who are near him or her, inadvertently overshadowing their radiance.

Chapter Three

● ● ●

Keeping the Job:
Revisiting First Impressions

Okay, so your first impression of your boss, and maybe even the company president, if you met her during your initial interview, was completely positive. You started your job filled with enthusiasm and hope. But somewhere along the way, maybe it was the second week, or the second month, things aren't as rosy as you initially thought. The person you report to still thinks you're terrific but the head of the company seems less than pleased with you. You consider what you've achieved since beginning this job and it's quite amazing, but it just isn't enough for the company president. (You reread Chapter 2 and realize you are working for The Vampire boss.) But you can't leave—you won't leave—since you need this job and you especially need at least six months or a year at the job so your resume doesn't make you look like a quitter.

The rest of this book will help you to survive the next few months or even the next year or two. But let's quickly look at a few additional strategies that will immediately help you out.

Strategy #8
Manage Expectations (Including Your Own "Honeymoon is Over" Letdown)

One of the first ways to help you keep your job is to manage everyone's expectations about what you are able to contribute to the company, especially in a short timeframe. Maybe you were brought in to transform a department, or generate more revenue or additional clients. Of course some of the expectations are warranted; some are unrealistic and trying to meet those demands is making it hard to face work everyday.

They may expect you to perform miracles but you have to help them to understand that what you do is a process, not an event.

Here are some helpful tips if you or someone you know is falling into the "honeymoon is over" mindset with their new work relationships:

- Just as the boss or coworkers were initially seen in a favorable light and now they are seen in the opposite way, the truth is probably somewhere in the middle. In time, those you work for or with will be viewed in a more tempered way.
- Their assessment of you is probably undergoing an adjustment as well.
- Since everyone goes through this process, having these letdown feelings does not mean that you made a mistake taking this job, or beginning a new work relationship.
- Your enthusiasm for the people and for your job itself will have ups and downs and that, too, is normal.

You may also want to decide if you are dealing with a "honeymoon is over" situation or if you work environment is truly toxic. Here is a self-quiz that might help you to make that determination:

QUIZ: RECOGNIZING A TOXIC WORKPLACE

1. Is your boss erratic and hard to please?
2. Were promises made when you were first hired that have still not been fulfilled, e.g., you were hired to replace someone else but that other employee is still doing your job?

3. Does your boss expect you to regularly work evenings and weekends without additional compensation?

4. Are there individuals working for the company who seem to be hired on the hiring manager (or owner's) whim?

5. Despite less-than-impressive revenues or sales figures, does your boss or the company's owner refuse to modify their business practices to more proven ways that might lead to greater profitability?

6. Do you find yourself wondering "What was I thinking?" when you initially accepted this position?

7. Do you notice a decided cooling towards you from either coworkers or your superiors?

8. Does the human resource department report to your boss so that you are unable to lodge any justified complaints about him/her?

If you answered "yes" to just one or two questions, your work situation might still be salvageable. However, you will need to make a concerted effort to better cope with, or try to reverse, the negative situations at your current job. (If you answered "yes" to all of the above questions, you might want to start dusting off your resume and, discreetly, begin a job search now.) The environment may be so toxic that it will be hard to deal with so many negative situations. But you can certainly still try; this book will help you to do that. Also, even if you do decide to look for a new job, it will probably help you in your next situation to understand what might be going on at your current toxic one.

If a particular relationship gets off on the wrong foot, refer to the strategies in the rest of this chapter to see why things may be out of kilter and the cause of the less than ideal start to this relationship. If you think some time needs to pass before you try again, that's fine.

Strategy #9
Be Humble (Humility Will Take You Further in Business Than Ego and Hubris)

Ever notice how many people say they didn't expect to win an award, and that just being nominated is as much of an honor, but then they whip out an acceptance speech that they obviously worked on intensively just "in case" they happened to win?

Everyone is expected to say, "What a surprise!" even if they secretly believe they are "the one" and "best," head and shoulders above their competition! How would it have sounded if someone blurted out, instead of their surprise that they won, their belief that "I knew I was going to win because I'm the best and the others are lucky that they were nominated so they at least had the thrill of temporarily being considered in the same class as me. But, alas, talent will out so I of course won."

The crowd and even the judges would probably regret that they gave that egotistical person the award in the first place. It's okay to think that you're great but watch out if you or someone at work or in business reeks of hubris through his or her words or actions.

An excellent model of humility is the awe-inspiring example of Captain Chesley "Sully" Sullenberger who accomplished the amazing feat of landing an airplane after a flock of birds took out both engines. Sullenberger made the split-second decision that he could not make it to another airport; his only chance was to land on the Hudson River, a feat never tried before with a passenger jet carrying 155 passengers and crew.

Sullenberger was successful and every single passenger and crew member survived that water landing, which could have been a horrific disaster. What impressed me in the first interview Sullenberger did with Katie Couric on *60 Minutes* was that Sullenberger admitted that he had trouble sleeping the first couple of nights after the incident. He was second-guessing himself, thinking over everything that happened and wondering what he could have done differently. Watching him express that concept to Couric was very humbling since Captain Sullenberger seemed to be concerned with his own view of his actions and the events rather than the triumphant regard of his choices by the media and the public.

HUMILITY AS TRUST

In our interview, Broadway producer Daryl Roth confirmed that humility will take you much further in her world of the theatre: "On the surface, you need to show your strength, your confidence and your surefootedness as you deal with the people you are working with. It is true that I am often feeling concern, insecure, and may question judgments from time to time, but on the surface, I try to appear confidence while I work through those issues. I am always willing to listen, discuss and compromise, but know that my role as a producer is to be a leader and remain in control. I always try to be respectful, and supportive of the people I work with. There is a lot to be said about being collaborative and humble."

Roth continues, "In theatre, we all have to have trust. We have to trust our director, actors have to trust their fellow actors. As a producer, I have to give over that trust and know that we are all working towards the same vision."

In this statement, Roth models how you can project confidence and competence without hubris when she adds, "I don't mean to be sound less than humble, but I feel I am a good producer and am very connected to the people I work with. I am very appreciative of their talent, gifts, and what they bring to the production."

Those with too big an ego probably do more to sabotage their ability to get along in the workplace or in business than any other character trait. If you have too much ego, others are less likely to want to get along with you because you will be perceived as self-centered, self-absorbed, and full of yourself rather than as part of a team effort. As the teacher at a training school for those who hoped to become professional athletes said at the beginning of the first class: "If you have an ego, drop it at the door or get the ——out."

Strategy #10
Avoid Upstaging Your Boss

Your job is to help your boss (and the company) to succeed whether that company consists of five, five hundred, or five thousand employees. But you want to accomplish that without upstaging your immediate boss or the head of the entire company, especially in public, and certainly you do not want to make yourself look good at your boss' expense.

There are some who say it is a generational issue when an employee, especially a new hire, tells the boss, or fellow coworkers, that he or she knows as much or more about the business as they do, or tries to be a "know it all." But my observation is that this tendency is more of a personality issue than a generational one. Perhaps the generational difference is that older workers who think they know as much as the boss, even on Day One, will keep that opinion to themselves; some younger workers may tell others they feel that way and one or two might even let the boss know that is how they feel.

Regardless of age, however, avoid trying to gather more limelight than your boss or even your company. Recently an executive was let go because of the economic downturn, but I also wondered if another reason is that she made her own name more prominent than the publication that she worked for. The principal of not upstaging the boss can refer to a person or to a brand or product as well. Today in most corporate environments, the focus is on doing what is best for the team or company.

Strategy #11
Emphasize Similarities Rather Than Focusing on Your Differences

Focus on what is similar rather than disparate between you and those you work with. Have you read the same books? Enjoyed the same movies? Of course it is fine to share about your varied tastes in music, magazines, or even the technology, but try to also find a common ground. Yes, it's popular to look at the difference, even to write books about it, such as *Men are from Mars and Women are from Venus,* as well as parodies of that concept. But at work, and in business, you will want to use that awareness and information to minimize rather than maximize the differences.

For example, if you are discussing work-related socializing with someone from Japan, who has told you that he spends two to three hours a week in after-work, business-related socializing, instead of saying, "I never spend that many hours a week socializing for business," you might point out, "We get together every couple of weeks for a drink on Fridays and we have our spring softball team that plays against rival companies."

So instead of dwelling on the number of hours that are dramatically different between the two businesspersons, the emphasis is on business socializing as a concept in which both participate.

Strategy #12
How Your Past Influences How You Deal With People

No one participates in a work situation as a *tabula Rosa*. We all bring our childhoods and previous work experiences to every new situation. Understanding the pushes and pulls will help you deal more effectively with others each day.

The same thing is true for your coworkers as well. Suppose that someone you depend on to do their job is acting very erratically. Their work has mistakes, which is unusual for this person. How would you find out what is behind this behavior? What is it in your background that will influence how you respond to the situation?

In business, you want to "know thyself." If others report to you, getting to know your coworkers, clients, customers, or service providers is time well spent as you will have a better understanding of why they make the decisions they make or why your interactions go the way they do. Obviously it is best to find out as much as possible about someone early on, since this is when most people find questions about their background are appropriate and expected.

But if you did not find out as much as you should have in the past, you can still take the time to find out more. Ask to have a cup of coffee or tea together, or go out for lunch. If you live far away, ask questions over the phone or through e-mail.

There is a condition known as *repetition compulsion*—the need to repeat a trauma until it is resolved. However, work is not the place to work out these issues; on your own or through therapy is where the change occurs. But you should be aware of whether you are being drawn into conflicts on the job because of common childhood/teen unresolved issues that play out at work:

- *"I keep finding my mother/my father/my sister/my brother."*

This is when you keep finding among your coworkers someone who seems to draw you back into your same negative relationships from childhood or the teen years, reviving the old unresolved issues.

- *"I can't take a compliment."*

This is when someone was criticized so often during their formative years that today, giving or receiving praise makes them feel uncomfortable. It means focusing on the negatives may become more of the norm, which can create a work atmosphere that is hypercritical. Yes, it's important to look at what can be improved but it is also key to point out what's positive.

- *"Don't be so negative."*

If someone grew up only hearing the negative, he or she could overcompensate today by emphasizing only the positive. This can be especially dangerous if the boss is the person who only wants to hear good news. By being "protected" from what is really going on, a department or even a company can slide down into ruination, which could have been prevented if the boss would have listened more openly about workplace problems and then taken measures to deal with them.

Strategy #13
Reassess your Work Relationships as Situations Change

You need to constantly review and relearn what you know about work relationships or specific individuals since people, times, and circumstances change. As you evolve at work, as well as change the type of work setting you find yourself in, you may want to reread this book, or take a course, as you find yourself facing different challenges. For example, right now you might be working for a major corporation with 100 to 1,000 employees but in two years, you might find yourself working alone from home with just one virtual assistant.

Have you recently gone from a working at home situation into a more traditional set up? If so, what are some of the differences in how you interact with peers that you need to consider if you are to hit the ground running in your new job? What if the opposite has happened: you have been asked to start working from home, or telecommuting, because the company is downsizing offices to save on its overhead. If you no longer have coworkers to talk to, or a boss nearby to directly report to, how will you restructure your day so you have the human interaction that may not be as readily available to you if you work at home day after day?

Strategy #14
Find a Way to Motivate Others to Want to Get Along With You

Make it advantageous to both of you to get along, remembering that everyone has his or her own agenda. Figure out what your and the other person's agenda is—the obvious and the hidden one—and where and how you can both accomplish what you need to/have to so it becomes a win-win relationship. What can you do to help the situation so that others like you and *want* you to succeed? How can you appeal to others on an emotional or business level so that you all want to work together? Find out what motivates the other person instead of looking at the world through your eyes only. For example, if someone only cares about your sales figures and not that you spent eighty dollars on a holiday basket as a gift; you had better focus on getting those numbers up in order to foster a stronger relationship with that individual.

One of the more frustrating aspects of relationships is that you cannot force someone to feel what you feel. This is true in affairs of the heart, in friendship, and in work relationships, whether in the workplace or in business. You have to do whatever you can to increase the likelihood that someone else will want to get along with you. As someone once said when he announced that he was ending their business relationship, "You can't make me want to be your..." Of course no one can "make" someone else want to work together or for each other, but you can certainly try to stack the cards in your favor by applying as many of the positive strategies to improving work relationships that are shared in this book with those you encounter at work or in business. These include being a good listener, dealing appropriately with your anger, not overreacting so that you are labeled a hot head, leaving your ego at the door, or being aware of your own childhood and prior work experience "baggage" that might lead you to be less than optimistic about the outcome in specific work relationships.

Strategy #15
Form Positive Bonds at Work

When you were in school, connections often happened naturally as an outgrowth of being in the same homeroom, class, or after school activity together. You saw each other in class, you observed interactions with others, and maybe you had a friend or two in common. You need to take that same "look and see" attitude at work when considering someone for a friend.

Watch for clues and cues, such as asking your work relationship out for a drink at the end of the work day, or for a cup of coffee, and see if the person you have just met at work seems to share your interest in becoming closer or if it is best to just remain acquaintances or coworkers. As noted later on in the section on oil and water (see Strategy #29 in Chapter 5) you may find you just do not "click" with someone. In your social life, that might be fine. You just move on and you find a way not to have to deal with that person again. But in the workplace, if that person is your coworker or supervisor, you may have to find a way to get along, whether or not you want to.

Or, if someone is pulling back from you, wait for a better time to try to move your relationship along. If someone's computer has broken down and she is stressed out and rattled, maybe you will want to avoid asking her out for lunch that day and just let her attend to her computer hassles.

Befriending at the same level is safest in the workplace or at business but sometimes there are status changes. For example, you start off at the same level, and you form a friendship but then, in time, one of you is promoted. Fortunately, some people are able to circumvent those changes (e.g., a boss who remains friends with her former coworkers who are now her subordinates). For most, however, it is necessary to choose between the new role of boss and friend.

If a coworker/friend goes to another company, or a client/friend moves to another country—how will they keep their relationship going now that they no longer work together? Will the relationship transcend those challenges or succumb to the diminished intimacy that often occurs because of the loss of that day-to-day work familiarity?

It is not just physical distance that can cause a relationship to erode. There are emotional changes that can form the basis of the decreasing connection. One of the most telling signs that your relationship is dwindling is withholding personal information, such as responding to "How are you?" by saying only "Fine," rather than giving a short but revealing answer; or by deliberately deciding not to share something meaningful that you share with others.

It is okay if a workplace relationship "de-evolves" back to the level of acquaintance. It is also okay if you find that your work relationship changes as status or work situations change. This is a natural filtering process. If you remained close or best friends with everyone you met at work or in business you might find you have little time or emotional energy for all the others in your life—your personal friends, romantic partner/spouse, children, extended family, and others. Reverting to a casual friendship or even an acquaintanceship is not a sign of trouble or defeat but the sifting out or shifting that occurs over a lifetime.

A work or business relationship completely ends. Why? Quite often it's just a circumstantial thing. One or both of you moves on. The relationship served its purpose while you were together or in the same field. That's okay. If both of you want to continue your relationship after your work association ends, make the time to do that. But avoid forcing it just because you always thought you "should" stay in communication. Relationships outside of work or business have to be sincere to work. Forcing connections once you no longer "have" to work together, or do business together, is uncomfortable. Yes, change is tough especially changes in relationships and the circumstances surrounding those relationships. But it can also be a positive opportunity to reassess your work or business relationships.

The rise of social networking sites and the application of those sites for business purposes, such as LinkedIn.com, Facebook.com, and others are helping workplace and work-related relationships to continue even on a minimal basis. (These social networking sites are fully discussed in Strategy #56 in Chapter 10.) As lifetime employment at one company becomes less and less likely internationally, maintaining as strong and current a work network for potential new opportunities may be worth the time and effort as long as it does not take up so much time that you are failing to do your current job, growing the business connections that are most timely and relevant.

What everyone wants to try to avoid, however, is ending a work relationship, including a friendship at work, because of a rift or feud. This can lead to a lot of stress and even career derailment if the feud becomes public and "everyone" knows that certain individuals do not want to work together. Whenever possible, keeping things on an amicable (or at least neutral) basis is much better than animosity (reciprocal or not) at a current or previous job or work situation.

Chapter Four

***

Developing Better Interpersonal
Communication Skills

Strategy #16
Going from "Me" to "We": Becoming More of a Team Player

Probably one of the biggest differences between working for a company and working as a solo entrepreneur or freelancer is the shift from a "me" to a "we" mentality if you are to be considered part of a team at work. It is not as simple as referring to what the company manufactures as "our" product. It is a mental and behavioral shift that needs to resonate in your daily work relationships and encounters.

Share the credit and make your other team members feel good. Be mindful that you are part of the team and that you are carrying your weight. Make sure every member of the team knows what their responsibilities are and fulfills them. You do not criticize other team members but you try to help them fulfill their job responsibilities because the success of the company depends on how well your team is doing.

For example, if you know that someone in your department is going on vacation at the end of the week, it will be in everyone's best interest to make sure that time-sensitive projects are completed or reassigned. There ought to be a system in place for communicating your coworker's absence through an e-mail auto responder or a prerecorded voice mail with suggestions about who is covering for him or her during that vacation time. Your coworker will look better if she or he also takes the time to advise customers, clients, or others at the company of his or her whereabouts, as well as what to do if anything arises during the upcoming absence. This will enable your team and even your department to be seen as part of a corporate team rather than as a collection of separate individuals doing their isolated jobs who just happen to share the same work space.

Here are some suggestions for teambuilding:

- Have a weekly lunch that everyone in the department attends. If possible, have management pick up the tab for the meal. Ordering-in pizza is an easy and cost-effective option.
- Have a quarterly, semi-annual, or annual retreat for the department or the company. Bring in outside speakers who discuss teamwork and have teambuilding activities, such as dividing up into groups and building something together, or creating a painting or a working on a project as a team.
- Create two teams within the company and have occasional team sports based on the season, such as baseball or volleyball in the spring or summer, and basketball or bowling in the winter.
- Copy and distribute readings on teamwork and get together as a department to discuss the issues that are raised.
- Celebrate each person's birthday in your department as a team with a cake or doughnuts.
- Have a holiday lunch or some way other way of celebrating the holidays or the New Year.

Strategy #17
Improve Your Conversational Techniques

One of my favorite parts of Dale Carnegie's classic book, *How to*

Win Friends and Influence People is where he shares about being seen as a good conversationalist. Quite simply, Carnegie defines the conversationalist as being the person who shows an interest in the other person by asking questions, expressing concern, and responding to his or her comments or statements. This is the direct opposite of the person who talks about himself or herself, whether out of self-absorption or nervousness. So the first step to improving your conversation techniques is to make sure you are, in fact, having a conversation with someone else and not just a monologue.

A conversation needs to be an exchange between the two, three, or four (or more) persons that are participating in the interaction. Too often, one person will dominate each conversation. Getting, or granting, equal air time to all the participants is one of the key challenges for someone who facilitates a group discussion.

In every conversation that you partake in, especially at work or in business, you need to be both one of the participants in the conversation as well as acting as if you are also a facilitator. If you think the other person is hogging the floor, interject and, without being too aggressive, take the floor back for yourself. If you see yourself dominating the discussion, step in and shift the focus to the other person or persons in the discussion. Ask questions such as, "And what do you think about it?" "So how's the weather in your neck of the woods these days?" "If you saw the movie *Slumdog Millionaire*, what did you think of it?" "What do *you* think of our latest vacation policy change?" or a similar question that shifts the emphasis from yourself to the other conversation participant.

COMMUNICATION ISSUES WITH
YOUR SUPERVISOR OR THE CEO

You do not want to shield vital information from your boss

or the company's CEO because that may cause your boss or the CEO to become part of a cocoon, losing out on precious insights and reality checks that could stave off disaster. You will always, therefore, walk the delicate line between risking criticism for bringing up unpleasant realities about the department, company, or industry and being thanked for having the foresight or courage to point out key issues that could help keep the company competitive, on track, and in the forefront.

COMMUNICATION PREFERENCES

One of the key questions you can ask someone in business is: how do you *prefer* to be contacted? In our personal lives we tend to know which of our friends are "phone people" and which ones hate the phone but love e-mail or even instant messaging. Why is it any different in business? There are those at work, or in business, who prefer one way of communicating over another. That does not mean that way is better or worse in general but, for that individual, it is the most comfortable or even the most efficient way to communicate with them.

If you take the time to find out what way is most simple and easiest for someone else, that will help you to get the best results. However, of course, if it is something urgent, even if you know your coworker prefers to get an e-mail, you may have to walk down the hall and ask him something face to face, or pick up the phone and call. Or if your e-mails are being ignored, you may have to call, especially with coworkers who work offsite or if you are in an international business and you are unsure if your e-mail is even getting through. You will need to find out what is going on —it could be a technological glitch—to get the answers that you need.

Strategy #18
Become a Better Listener

Here is an acronym I developed that helps to remind us all about what it is to be an effective listener:

L – Look someone in the eye when he or she speaks.

I – Indicate you are listening by nodding your head when you agree, smiling, or other gestures.

S – Show interest by reframing what someone has said or by asking questions about what you just heard.

T – Taking the time to listen makes your coworker feel deserving and valued in a positive and respectful way.

E – Empathy about what your coworker is saying will get you farther than criticism or judgment.

N – Never interrupt your coworker (or boss) before he or she has finished a sentence or is completing his or her thought or point. Try to avoid looking at your watch or a clock in an obvious way that might make him or her feel that you're bored or dismissive.

Improving your listening will take you far in business. If you are prone to talking rather than listening it is going to take some effort to break this habit. But it is a habit that can be broken. By listening to what someone else is saying, and by asking questions, you are showing an interest in someone else. Self-interest is a basic principle upon which individuals operate; it is only human. If you show interest in another, you are fanning that person's self-interest and deflecting some of the attention from your own self-preoccupation to another. By listening, and showing a concern for others, you avoid the label of narcissist (not a positive trait or label in most traditional workplace or work situations).

Some are constantly talking, whether about topics or themselves, out of nervousness. They really do not mean to seem so self-centered but especially when they are in a face-to-face situation, they run at the mouth, so to speak. If you have this tendency, be aware of it and try hard to fight against it when you are in those situations, especially one-on-one over coffee or lunch or in a meeting. Those who tend to do this may retreat from face-to-face meetings and instead "meet" by phone or through e-mail. This is a way to avoid being labeled a "talker" but it also can deny you the chance to benefit from the positive aspects of getting together in person if you can just overcome your tendency to dominate conversations.

Remember that allowing for silences in a conversation is part of the listening experience. It means that you are considering what someone is saying. You are also pacing your communication with someone else, having a true back-and-forth that is thoughtful and considered rather than something as automatic as a tennis or volleyball volley.

Here are other suggestions shared in a more detailed way to help you with the all-important skill of listening more effectively at work to your coworkers as well as to anyone at work or in business:

- Concentrate on what someone is saying when he or she talks to you.
- Catch yourself if your mind is wandering when you are supposed to be listening and bring your attention back to the speaker.
- It helps to restate what someone has said in your own words to show that you have really heard him or her. If it seems comfortable, you might reframe what you have just heard. For example, if your coworker tells you that the deadline for delivery 10,000 units of a certain product is unrealistic you might reply, "So you're telling me that we need to rethink the deadline for those 10,000 units."
- Avoid thinking about what you are going to say next instead of focusing on what someone is saying to you.

- Listen without judgment. Only give your opinion if you are asked for it.

- Allow enough time for someone to talk to you so you do not cut short your listening because you are withholding information, or out of fear that you will have to leave.

- Avoid being critical because that will probably cause your coworkers to start withholding information out of fear that you will disapprove. Before you know it, you might find yourself out of the loop with your department which could have negative consequences on your how well you can perform your job.

- Be sensitive to the emotions behind your coworker's words, not just the words.

- Observe the nonverbal communication that is shared— the body language, the facial gestures—not just the words. Even if you are communicating via e-mail, you can see if there are symbols added to the e-mail, indicating a state of mind.

- Show interest by asking questions.

- Avoid interrupting.

- Avoid switching the subject in an abrupt way. Have a natural bridge from topic to topic and make sure your coworkers has stopped talking is and is ready to go on to the next topic. If you absolutely have to switch topics abruptly, use that as your bridge. "I hate to switch the subject but…." or, "Turning to a completely different topic…."

- Demonstrate active listening by maintaining eye contact or by nodding your head when you agree—but not nodding your head so much that you seem more like a Bobble Head doll!

Strategy #19
Become a Better Storyteller

Whether you want to appear on a major talk show to get exposure for your services or products, or you want to forge a relationship with your coworker or boss, becoming a better storyteller will help you to accomplish these goals. Your storytelling ability will help you to stand out from the pack. It is a way to be remembered and to make that connection that could be the initial spark to a relationship.

When I do a workshop, as an ice breaker, I sometimes will ask my audience to think about one thing that no one in that room knows about them, something that will surprise everyone. (I caution them not to pick something that will embarrass them.) We then go around the room and it is always amazing what each person shares; the better they are as storytellers, the more likely they will stand out from the dozens in that audience. I recall one speaker in the audience in Auckland, New Zealand who shared that her secret ambition was to become a stand-up comedian. It was a memorable goal and story.

You might want to apply this technique to your company, if you are an entrepreneur. What can you say about your company or services that will distinguish it from all the others so that someone remembers you and wants to do business together/start a business relationship? If you are looking to hire someone, what is unique about your company so that others will want to work there? Practice your answers on others; see if you get the positive response that you are looking for.

Strategy #20
Use Reciprocity in Conversations and Relationships

If Bob asks you how you're feeling and you answer, and you ask

Bob how he is feeling, and Bob replies, that's reciprocity in a conversation. Or, Beth shares about a project she is working on, and then asks you about your project, or you volunteer the information.

Sometimes the instinctive need for reciprocity in conversation can be manipulated in a situation so that someone shares what should not be shared. For example, there are some interviewers who are known to get very chatty with those they interview, sharing their own secrets, hoping that those they interview will do the same. Often the interviewees do just that, but when their reciprocal comments are published, it causes much embarrassment, and it's not the same thing as publishing an untruth.

Here's another example of how reciprocity works. Someone shares about their family. You share about yours. There's some good news that you're sharing. That leads to an e-mail back, congratulating you. The reciprocity concept is most apparent when someone breaks the "rule." For example, you share and the other person does not share back, or they fail to congratulate you for good news, and suddenly, it is as if the "universe" is out of alignment, or the karma has been thrown off. Often, that person is too important in your job or career for you to say anything. You know it would backfire since, sadly, when you share with others even though you think you're helping by sharing your feelings, the reciprocity theme kicks in again and, at some point, they might do something to make you feel just as awkward as your "sharing" made them feel. However, if the integrated conflict management system (see Strategy #27 in Chapter 5) is put in place, then you will be able to share and give feedback without fear of reprisal or reprimand.

Here's another example of negative reciprocity at work: you are late to a meeting. The next time you have a meeting with this individual, they are late so now you are kept waiting. Coincidence?

Strategy #21
Become a Better Networker

FACE-TO-FACE NETWORKING

Becoming the kind of networker who develops and maintains positive relationships at work and in business has a lot to do with being a good listener; there is a strong connection between the two concepts.

For many, the term "networking" is a misnomer. What is really sought after is a one-on-one relationship.

Networking, by contrast, means that individuals start off separately but the networking process takes those disparate individuals and helps them to evolve into a fully integrated "network." In the pre-social networking online days, I interviewed a woman from Texas once who arrived in New York City for a job; she quickly looked up one or two former classmates at college who were also from Texas. Within a short period of time, by adding the friends of friends and growing the network, it expanded into dozens of contacts. All of those contacts were face-to-face.

Michael Hughes is an Ottawa, Ontario, Canada-based expert on networking. His company, NFR Consulting Group, helps individuals to improve their networking techniques as a business strategy. I first met Michael at a networking event for speakers around the world organized by the Global Speakers Network that included a tour of the United Nations in New York City and a dinner afterwards. Practicing what he preaches, Michael spends more than three hours a week socializing for business purposes. These are the activities that he engages in: networking events such as the Ottawa Chamber of Commerce meetings (a combination of breakfasts, lunches, after work gatherings or dinners); and various business groups, such as a recent Texas Hold 'Em charity event put on by a small business. He selectively attends other business network events when there's a speaker he wants to hear, individuals he wants to meet, or he has been asked to speak, himself.

What's Michael's favorite way to network? He replies: "Networking is just one-on-one contact. I see a networking event like a Chamber of Commerce event as a series of one-on-one connections as a starting point to create the spark to have that further one-on-one connection. It allows me to connect with more people more quickly so in making those connections I can choose which of those connections I feel will have more potential, and leverage them into the one-on-one coffee or lunch that I feel will help that relationship to blossom."

What got him interested in networking? "Survival. I had a small business I started 17 years ago and I was rapidly starving to death. More often than not, when I connected with people one-on-one I was able to elicit needs that people had but I couldn't meet enough people fast enough to grow my business to the level that I needed. The sales process is a filtering process. You might meet five people and you agree to submit a proposal to three to get one client. I didn't have enough background or traction to get to enough people." So Michael asked himself: "Is there a way I can meet more people faster? [At his first networking event] there were forty people. I thought I had died and gone to heaven. At a three-hour event I could meet between ten and twenty people. Then I started to study the process. Looking at those connections as a starting point, I started to research networking as a strategy, as a way to grow the business whether it's a sales professional, business professional or even corporate professional."

I asked Michael about clients whose careers have taken off by working with him. He shared one example:

> "There was an executive VP of a large multinational corporation based here in Toronto. Part of his issue was he wanted to get up one level. He was executive vice president and he wanted to have the top position in Canada of general

manager of the Canadian operation. His issue was that he didn't have the skill-set to manage and maximize and leverage the relationships in his peer group. What he and I did was reevaluate what he was doing with each of those relationships within his peer group and refine each of those relationships. What was he contributing and how could he use those strategies to better leverage himself and support him when the time came for the transition to support him in the corporate hierarchy? In a six- to twelve-month period of his evaluating the relationships of the people he was working with and investing in those relationships, he built trust and had those people renew their trust in him. It took six to twelve months for that to take place. If you're serious out it, this is a 12- to 36-month process. Relationships take time, require investment, and need to be nurtured."

How did the process work? They initially spoke on the phone once or twice a week during the first month to map out the strategy the executive would be following in his networking efforts within the company. Says Michael: "We developed a structure around each of the relationships: where he was, where he was going, and how much further he needed to go with each one." After that first month, they talked every two weeks unless there was an emergency debriefing because of a meeting that was coming up. "The first month to three months, there's much more contact as he developed his confidence and understood the principles by keeping moving forward and keeping the momentum going."

Like work relationships, networking is not going to be a static skill throughout your work experiences. It will evolve as you evolve and your work and work relationships change. Broadway producer Daryl Roth comments on how her networking efforts and activities evolved as her career has developed over the last 22 years: "In the beginning, I really searched out projects, play readings and opportunities for myself. I was a new kid on the block and nobody knew I was here. My ears and eyes were open as I went to play readings and began meeting people, agents, writers, and fellow producers. Now, many years later and after producing many plays, the process is much different. Playwrights, actors, directors, agents, and other producers will call to interest me in their projects. I welcome hearing from those in the industry with whom I have worked before about working on a new project. I love working with people over and over again once relationships of trust and partnering have been formed."

Networking is fortunately a skill that can be mastered through trial and error, observing, and studying what works and what does not. Being self-confident and realizing that you don't have to say everything about yourself or try to win over everyone in the room can help you to be more relaxed and approachable in an in-person networking opportunity. Sometimes if you walk into a room full of people, instead of trying to get to know as many people as possible, try to start with one, introduce yourself, spend enough time to strike a common ground with that person, exchange business cards, and move on to the next. If you meet even one person with whom you feel there is a strong and positive connection, it will be a worthwhile investment of your time. If you spend ten or fifteen minutes with a couple of new people, you can meet and expand your horizons by as many as four to six people in just one hour. It is better to meet and connect with one person, and initiate one positive new relationship, than to turn off, or to be considered obnoxious, by many.

TWELVE THINGS *TO AVOID* DOING WHEN NETWORKING

1. Coming on too strong.
2. Being excessively boastful.
3. Doing all the talking rather than asking questions and listening.
4. Acting too angry.
5. Being so shy you keep to yourself and don't interact at all.

6. Badmouthing others.
7. Pushing your company or product on to others whether they show an interest or not.
8. Failing to introduce those you already know to someone new that you meet.
9. Acting desperate.
10. Telling perfect strangers too much information.
11. Sharing opinions on politics, religion, or other controversial topics that lead to arguments and head butting.
12. Being a know-it-all.

Strategy #22
Handle Difficult Conversations

Words need to be carefully chosen in the workplace and in business because words are either motivators or sources of discouragement—and words are remembered. This is especially true when a difficult conversation is involved. Difficult conversations are usually related to negative feedback about performance, whether a subordinate about a boss, or a boss or supervisor about an employee. Coworkers, too, have difficult conversations with each other, especially if it refers to something such as shared space or a shared project.

Here's some advice from Jim Smith, CEO of Enterprises Management Group, a Sammamish, Washington-based consultant who goes in and helps companies to save money while still saving jobs. Practically every conversation he has when he generates new business and then goes in and does each project is a difficult conversation. But Jim has found that taking a Dale Carnegie course in interpersonal relations and communication skills when he was younger has helped him throughout his career. "It helps me to this day," Jim confirms. What's the key concept that he learned about handling difficult conversations? As Jim explains: "When you're building a relationship, and especially if you know it's likely going to be an adversarial one, everything you're saying is a question rather than a statement. Before I took the course, I would go in and yell at someone. Now, instead, I will just listen to other people and let them tell me what happened and in due course they explain what they did wrong. This approach almost always results in a friendlier and more professional relationship surviving beyond the incident."

Here are some additional challenging situations. What might you say to make the situation less difficult?

- A coworker returns from a few days off for personal reasons.
- You have to cancel getting together on Friday after work.
- You decided you don't have the time to do an informational interview with your coworker's nephew.
- A colleague is being promoted instead of you.

The rule of thumb is to say to another that which you might want said to you in a difficult conversation. However, always look out for body language and try to know as much as possible about the background of the other person so you can take those cues and differences into account in how you handle it.

- Situation: I notice that you're distracted lately. Is something going on?
  — Take responsibility for your behavior. Give reasons why it's been happening. Apologize and provide reassurance it will not happen again. If you are in the supervisory role, explain why your employee's state of being distracted puts everyone at risk. What are the ways to improve the situation? What will the consequences be if it does not improve?

- Situation: We are unable to give you a bonus this year because of the budgetary problems we are facing but we want you to know that your work has still been outstanding.
  — If this is told to you, be humble and gracious even if you would prefer more money to the praise.
  — You might want to give your employee hope that when things improve financially, you will not forget his superior work and you will find a way to reward him/her financially as soon as it is possible.
- Situation: Why have you been coming in late so often in the last month or so?
  — In your explanation, share why you have been late but also take responsibility for being so irresponsible and emphasize that it won't happen again.
  — If you are the boss or supervisor asking the question, try to point out how the lateness impacts on the entire team and the company as well as on your employee's reputation for consistency. Also, note the potential consequences in terms of getting a harsher evaluation or even being docked in pay.

In both instances, try to adopt a "How could we avoid this happening in the future?" approach rather than behaving in an authoritarian manner.

Strategy #23
Ten Things You Should Never Share With a Workplace Relationship

Here are ten things to avoid sharing in the workplace or with a business relationship that will help your interpersonal communication:

1. Business confidences that would be a violation of trust and ethics if revealed to anyone.
2. Family secrets that put someone else in your family in any level of jeopardy.
3. Naming names about your romantic affairs, whether current or past.
4. If your spouse (or romantic partner) is good in bed.
5. Anything you would not feel comfortable having repeated on the six o'clock news or reading about in a national newspaper.
6. Any negative feelings about the boss (co-worker, company president, customer, or client).
7. Comments that are racist, sexist, anti-aging, or against any religion or culture.
8. Negative comments about a colleague's family member, especially if those reactions are subjective and if the behavior is not dangerous nor illegal.
9. Making unfounded promises such that defaulting would disappoint your coworker's family members, especially children, such as offering to get tickets to a sports event, concert, or celebrity gala.
10. Blurting out whatever you think when asked your opinion on politics, current events, or "charged" situations without considering how those viewpoints may be received or perceived. (Some might find it entertaining to watch, but it can be uncomfortable to have to work with someone with whom the tempers flare.)

Chapter Five

● ● ●

Getting Along Better

T*here are certain behaviors* that you can try to put into practice at work and in your business so that you are less likely to annoy others. I am talking about having the positive traits of being on time, having a desk that is organized and neat, avoiding procrastination so you are less likely to incur the wrath of coworkers or bosses who are waiting for your materials, or customers who are eager to get your product.

Strategy #24
Be Considerate in All Your Dealings With Others

Want to annoy someone? Just show up an hour late for an appointment. That will certainly make most people furious—if they're still around when you finally arrive.

If you are going to be late, pick up the phone and call. If something comes up and you have to reschedule a phone call or a meeting—and emergencies or other priorities do occur—let the other person know as soon as you realize a change is necessary. If you absolutely can't get to a phone, or there is no cell phone service where you are calling from, at least get back to that person as soon as you can and apologize for the missed appointment. A little "I'm sorry" with a plausible and honest explanation can go a long way to head off anger and resentment. (But if you cancel on someone, even if you tell them in advance, do not be completely surprised if you find he or she cancels you once or twice after that. That's a negative aspect of the "reciprocity" rule I mentioned before.)

Despite your best efforts, if you do get off to a rocky start with someone at work, or if you started off okay but something has happened to shift your relationship in a negative way, deal with it right away. Ignoring the negativity rarely works since the relationship problems may fester or multiply and it is usually harder to undo a negative start down the road. There is no need to be confrontational, but, ignoring the situation generally is not a productive option.

Strategy #25
Be a Principled Person

1. Have mutual respect. You're not the only one trying to make things work at the office even though it's human nature to be more focused on your own career and your own advancement than anyone else's.
2. Share a commitment to getting along with each and everyone you work with or that you report to.
3. Understand the boundaries to the relationship as defined by each participant in the relationship and keep those boundaries in mind.
4. Keep all confidences, work-related and personal.
5. Deal with conflicts or disagreements immediately and appropriately.
6. Avoid holding a grudge even if you were right and you were wronged.
7. Make sure someone earns your trust before you share something that could be used against you or shared indiscriminately even if done by accident or in jest.
8. Before you get offended or angry, listen to the other person's explanation or perspective. There may be facts or extenuating circumstances you do not know about that help explain a situation that you misconstrued.

9. Emphasize your similarities and shared goals, interests, values, or beliefs rather than creating a wedge by dwelling on your differences.

10. Share credit, as appropriate, so you get labeled a "we" not just a "me" colleague.

Strategy #26
Become Skilled at Connecting and Caring

Whether you work in a company with ten employees, or 10,000, it is the ability to connect one-on-one, and to make each person you meet by e-mail, phone, or in-person feel as if he or she really matters, that can make all the difference in whether or not you succeed, especially if you are in a job that requires people skills. (Even if you are in a job that relies on technical skills, such as medicine, you may find yourself losing patients if they do not feel that you care about them personally, no matter how superior your scientific skills may be.)

Pat Schroeder, former congresswoman from Colorado who retired undefeated and who went on to become president and CEO of the Association of American Publishers (AAP) for twelve years until she retired in 2009, was an executive who had the uncanny ability to make those she met or dealt with in her job feel as if they mattered. How did Pat manage to answer every e-mail and return every phone call by the end of the work day? Excellent time management skills helped, of course. Delegating to a reliable executive assistant who passed along to others at the association the e-mails or phone calls that they should attend to rather than Pat also made it easier. As Pat said in an interview: "I learned in politics that time is your most precious asset and if you can deal with something right away, rather than read it over several times and push it aside, it works much better. Also it is very helpful to have staff that you've known for a long time and that knows you. That way you are much more comfortable delegating things to them. Having staff that knows what you are interested in really helps. There never are enough hours in the day, so using the ones that are there efficiently is absolutely essential!"

Connecting one-on-one is key to getting along at work whether you are working in a small business or campaigning to become the next president of the United States. For example, Randy Wehrman was a life-long Republican who ultimately cast his vote for President Barack Obama, a Democrat, because Obama had made Randy feel that he cared about him and his late wife, Beth. Beth, an early Obama volunteer and supporter from Iowa, cast her vote a month in advance of the election because she thought she might not make it till Election Day since she was battling terminal pancreatic cancer. Over the year that Beth and Randy fought cancer—Randy had prostate cancer—Obama kept in communication with the Wehrmans. He even asked Randy Wehrman to introduce him at a political event in Davenport, Iowa in August 2008. Obama kept in communication with the Wehrmans throughout their tough year. In Kathy Kiely's *USA Today* article about Obama's bond with the Wehrmans, she quotes Randy Wehrman as saying, after Obama called to offer his support when Beth passed away: "'For a guy that busy to care about us, it was like—wow.'"

Caring is a trait that can help catapult you to the top of your department, your company, or even your industry. Getting known as someone who cares about your coworkers and business associates will take you far in your career. Even if you have to take the time to write holiday cards on an airplane on your way back from a business trip, or buy a token birthday present for your top customer during your rushed half-hour lunch, showing that you care, especially if it is heartfelt, is one strategy that definitely helps strengthen relationships at work and in business.

Strategy #27
Reexamine Your Attitude Toward Conflict

How sweet it would be and how simplistic if we could all avoid conflict with our coworkers and business associates. Is that possible? Is it feasible? The Conflict Management Approach to Conflict, as labor expert Deborah Katz of the Transportation Security Administration points out, is to see conflict as inevitable. The key is in how to deal effectively with it, *not* to bemoan the presence of disputes or conflicts. Yes, it would be "nice" to avoid conflicts in the first place, but how you handle conflict is key since it is unrealistic to avoid it all together.

In their presentation, "Beyond ADR: Integrated Conflict Management Systems," Jennifer Lynch, Q.C., PDG People Development Global Inc. and Deborah Katz explore "the next generation of conflict management" known as the Integrated Conflict Management System (ICMS). This shift in approach was first implemented in Canada, the World Bank, and the Australia Defence Organisation. The change in terminology and perspective is the shift from "ADR" and "dispute resolution" to "conflict management." According to Lynch and Katz, conflict encompasses these four critical situations:

1. Employee and supervisor disputes
2. Peer conflicts
3. Issues and tensions that drain productivity
4. Problem solving by people with varying points of view

With the goal of "a culture of conflict competence," the "integrated conflict management system" is based on "instead of handling disputes on a case-by-case basis, the organization shifts to a systematic focus on relationship management through the prevention, management and early resolution of conflict at the lowest possible level."

Conflict competence is defined in this way: "…People have confidence raising any issue or concern, knowing that it will be respectfully received and responsibly dealt with."

In our interview, Jennifer Lynch, formerly a consultant on the integrated conflict project and now a senior official with the Canadian government, summarized this different approach to conflict: "You recognize that conflict is normal. You have the concept of the conflict competent organization and the conflict competent leader. It has to do with how people treat each other and how decisions are made. How problems are managed or resolved."

These are the 4Rs to the conflict management approach and the conflict competent organization:

Recognize that people have different points of view and that something might cause conflict.
Respond to what has happened.
Resolve what needs to be resolved; determine what techniques will be used to resolve it.
Reflect on the lessons that were learned and how we can do it better.

What's unique about the conflict competent organization, as Jennifer Lynch points out, is that "you make conflict management a core competency."

The vital principle of this approach is: "Every individual can raise any idea, issue, or concern and know that it will be respectfully received and responsibly addressed."

Strategy #28
Follow "Fighting Fair" Rules if You Do Have a Conflict

Sometimes you will meet someone at work, or through business, and you find yourself in a heated argument or fight. He or she might start it, and as hard as you try to turn the other cheek, you are pulled into it, nevertheless. It would of course be nice if your coworker adheres to the same "fighting fair" rules but even if he or she does not, you should know these rules and follow the rules yourself:

- No physical actions whatsoever including no hitting, spitting, hair pulling, throwing furniture, or getting too close to someone with a finger that's shaking that could be considered menacing.
- Agree to disagree. There can be two points of view and each one could have equal merit.
- Agree to a "time out" or "cooling off" period so you can both reassess what has happened in a calmer and more rational frame of mind.
- Use the "I" approach to letting your colleague know that his or her behavior hurts you: "When you do this I feel _____." The emphasis is on how *you* feel rather than pointing out what the other person is doing is wrong.
- Avoid gossiping about the fight with others, but do share the situation, in confidence, with someone in authority if you think that step is warranted.
- If you used to be work friends and now you are arch enemies, keep the confidences that you shared with each other during your friendship (unless any of those secrets put you, your family, or the company at risk).
- If you do blurt out the confidences that were shared with you when your relationship was better, you may be seen as distrustful or disloyal, traits that can sabotage you in your work or personal relationships.
- If you feel you were wrong, or if you feel an apology will help the situation, consider giving one even if you are both at fault.

- No name calling including racial, ethnic, religious, or sexist slurs. Speak directly and avoid sarcasm. Listen to your opponent; don't just talk.

Strategy #29
Face Up to the "Oil and Water" Phenomenon

Apply this very simple test to each situation where you feel as if you're up against an oil and water work relationship in which you and the other person are just opposites, not getting along, and there's nothing specific you can point to that may have caused a rift. Ask yourself: is it him or her, or is it me?

If your answer is that you did not say or do anything that should have triggered such a negative response, then it is probably something in this person's history or unconscious that is causing the oil and water reaction. That said, how do you now handle it?

You might want to avoid dealing with this person and if you are self-employed or a freelancer, you might be able to eliminate this person as a vendor, client/customer, or service provider. But if you work in a traditional office setting, you probably have to find a way to get along since, at least for the time being, neither one of you will be leaving the job.

One approach is to try to bring out what is going on, making the unconscious conscious, so you and your coworker can somehow break through it. If you want to follow this approach, the next time this person makes a comment or performs an unprovoked action that demonstrates negative feelings toward you, you could try saying: "You seem to have a lot of very strong negative feelings about what I just said (or did). Are you aware that this is coming from you? I didn't do anything that I know of to provoke you. If I did something that has upset you or caused you to feel this way, let me know so we can discuss it and work this out."

Emphasize that you have to work together—or you share a common business goal—and that having a positive relationship without any residual animosity is in everyone's best interest.

"How can I help you so we can work together more amicably? Is there anything I could say or do differently so you're not so upset with me?"

Another approach is to force yourself to dwell on what is positive and beneficial in your oil and water colleague despite your differences. See this annoying relationship as an opportunity for your own growth. This is the strategy that Coach Augusta Nash used when she had to deal with an oil and water situation when she recently worked on a project with someone who was a "determined aggressive female." As Nash explains: "She was very trying. She very seldom thought about people's feelings when moving forward. She was less relationship-oriented than I am. I automatically cringed from her but had to work with her for six months."

So how did Nash continue to work with her despite their differences? Nash continues: "I kept having to remember that she had gifts that I didn't have. I was there to temper her gifts and she was there to elicit my gifts because I'm not terribly aggressive. Because she was my coworker, I could not make her wrong or I would diminish our reputation in front of the client. When I did talk to her, I told her what I did notice about myself and what I needed from her so I wouldn't overreact. I kept it about me."

Strategy #30
Use the Power of the Apology if You Have Done Something Wrong

Lauren M. Bloom is a Washington, D.C.-based lawyer who specializes in the apology and has even written a book on the topic, *The Art of the Apology*. What got Bloom interested in apologizing? She knew, as research about doctors has shown, that people are less likely to sue if there is an apology. Her book provides advice on why it's important to maintain good relations with bosses, colleagues, subordinates, clients and customers by admitting to human error when it occurs and by offering effective apologies. According to Bloom, it's imperative to create an "apology-friendly workplace" which she defines as "an environment where employees are free to admit to their own errors and help others, including their bosses, to catch and correct mistakes before they do lasting damage."

What's your attitude toward apologizing? Do you see it as a sign of weakness or as an admission that you are human and that you made a mistake? When was the last time someone apologized to you? Did you take that apology graciously, "apology accepted," or were those just words you uttered but you really still held a grudge?

Strategy #31
Deal With the "Back Off" Before it Turns Antagonistic

Have you ever experienced one or more of these situations at work?

- You agree to work together on a project—you even have this person's commitment in writing—but now he won't answer your e-mails. You are being ignored.
- You used to communicate on a regular basis but now you can't remember the last time you heard from a particular individual.
- You received half of your fee up front and the project is now completed. You are supposed to receive the second half of the fee but communication between you and your client has become one-way, even though he initially happily accepted your work.

- You and your coworker used to be friendly toward each other but lately you've felt like you're getting the cold shoulder.

These are just a few of the many examples of what I call The Back Off, a very annoying phenomenon in business that has become increasingly widespread. Rather than have a confrontation, someone backs off. Rather than risk having a discussion that might be unpleasant, there is no communication. Rather than rejecting a person or a project, there is silence. (The example above, the backing away from an agreed-upon fee, will be dealt with in Strategy #40 in Chapter 6.)

What causes the back off and what should you do about it? Ignore it? Confront it? Try to turn it around? The first step is to figure out why the back off might have occurred. Is the person busy? Did something happen between you that could be going on?

Here are some reasons that the back off is happening:

- You took too long to return this person's phone call, or e-mail, and now he or she, consciously or not, is determined to make you wait.
- This person is very busy and just can't get to you for now (but he or she doesn't know how to say that politely so avoiding you seems to be the better option.).
- This person has not received your phone call or e-mail because he or she is on vacation, no longer at that job, or has unwittingly erased or ignored your message.
- You are just not on this person's radar screen right now.
- This person is truly overwhelmed and swamped and he or she just can't get through the hundreds of e-mails or dozens of voice mails that need to be dealt with. Only urgent or priority communications are being acknowledged.

- You angered this person, and he or she does not know how to tell you.

You probably want to avoid a dramatic confrontation with the back off because you can't "make" someone want to deal with you just by pressuring them or bombarding them with calls or e-mails. But you can certainly try to increase their motivation to deal with you.

Here are some suggestions for dealing with the back off:

1. Try to communicate in another way. If you usually e-mail back and forth and your e-mails are being ignored, try picking up the phone and calling. It is amazing how often this simple change in how you communicate, even internationally and across time zone, can break through the back off.

2. Give someone the benefit of the doubt. There could be things going on in the business or personal life of your associate that are causing him or her to back off and it could have nothing to do with you. Be patient but still try to keep the communication going even if it seems to be more one-way than two-way for a while. Without being a gossip or a spy, see if you can find out from other sources such as reading any updates about this individual in the media or on the social networking sites that you both belong to that might help you understand why the communication has stopped. Perhaps he or she has just been laid off, is on maternity or medical leave, or is on a seven-week business trip without access to e-mail or the phone.

3. Send another communication in another format and without laying a guilt trip on your associate, just letting him or her know that you would like to hear back when he or she has the time.

4. Instead of just sending a "what's up" type of communication, or message, have something new and timely to share. For example, send an article or a piece of information that might be useful so you keep the information flowing without being overbearing.

5. If you work together, see if you can get together in person, for lunch or for a drink, to reestablish communication. If you do business together and you are far away from each other, still try to set up an in-person meeting, even if it's down the road at an upcoming conference or trade show that you are both attending.

6. Shift your energies to finding someone else to deal with instead of obsessing on the back off. In time, this person may get back to you and pick up where you left off, or explain why he or she backed off, or the contact may be lost forever. But at least you are moving your business and career along rather than continuing to fixate on him/her.

7. Help this person out showing in a concrete way that you care about this person and want to assist him or her in succeeding. Send business his way, offer to write a recommendation at one of the social networking sites, or even send a copy of a book or article you have read recently letting this person know that you found it enlightening and you thought he might, too.

THE SILENT TREATMENT

This is a variation of the back-off and must be handled just as sensitively.

The silent treatment is one workplace strategy to avoid—it is impolite, it can truly anger people, and most importantly, it is cruel. Of all the ways to end a relationship, being ignored is (arguably) the one that generates the most negativity. The silent treatment is when someone you have been regularly exchanging e-mails with stops returning your most recent e-mail. Your phone calls are ignored as well.

What should you do if someone does the silent treatment toward you?

- Try to connect with them in another way than you usually do. If your e-mails are ignored, try to send a fax. If you fax is ignored, try to set up an event or a required business interaction that will motivate them, or draw them out, so you can resume communications.
- Don't take it personally, even though it feels all too personal. They are either busy, stressed out, there are things brewing behind the scenes you are not privy to, and unfortunately too many are feeling that saying nothing is better than saying something that might be wrong.
- Get the hint that things are not going well for you with this person or these individuals and that company and start looking for new contacts, jobs, projects, or work connections that will be responsive and mutually beneficial.

Strategy #32
Get Over Hurt or Enraged Feelings

This can be a very tough call to make. Do you share with a fellow employee or client that he or she has offended you, or do you let it ride? There are pros and cons to each reaction.

The Pros to Sharing Your Hurt Feelings
- You will get it off your chest.
- If you are obsessing about it, sharing may help you to stop obsessing so you will be able to go back to focusing on your work.

- You will let the other person know what he or she said or did to upset you which might be a learning lesson to prevent a similar result with others.
- You will be seen as a sensitive and genuine person.

The Cons of Opening up About Your Feelings
- Revealing your deepest feelings and being seen as sensitive in some work settings could be misinterpreted as a sign of weakness.
- You may be giving the person you are complaining to too much power over you.
- If it turns out that you misinterpreted what was said or done, you may make a comment, situation, or action even more important than it would have been by dwelling on it, discussing it, and giving it more weight by bringing it up again.
- You may be judged as someone who is unable to easily deal with conflicts or that you overreact to words or actions that most others would take in stride.

Stopping Yourself From Hitting the "Send" Key When You're Upset

In the old days, when everyone relied on mailing letters to share in writing what they thought or felt, by the time you wrote the letter, put it in an envelope, filled out the address, found a stamp, and walked to the mailbox, you may have had a change of heart and torn up the letter instead of sending it. (If you put it in your "out" box, you probably had at least an hour or more before the mail was picked up so you could retrieve your letter from that box and no one would have been the wiser for it.) But now, with e-mail providing an instantaneous way to communicate, it is up to you to exercise the self-control and good judgment about when or if you should send an irate e-mail communication.

In terms of business protocol, the rule I have been advocating since I have been writing and speaking in this area for more than two decades is: praise in writing, criticize in person or, if it's at a distance, over the phone. Whenever possible, follow that rule. Criticism or angry words in writing, especially in an e-mail, might enflame the situation since the e-mail can be read over and over again, causing additional pain, but it can also intentionally or inadvertently be shared with others, making what should have been a private disagreement or dispute a public put-down or disagreement.

If you are thinking of writing, and sending, a negative e-mail to someone, instead of composing it in your e-mail software, instead write it on your computer in a separate program, not hooked up to the Internet. Save the text and promise yourself you will take some time to let your message sit. Return to it a few hours or even days later. If you still feel the same way, after you have reread your angry words with a less enraged heart, and you still want to send the message, with a clear head, you can do so. But you have given yourself the gift of time to reevaluate if this is the right thing to do or, if you still need to say those things, if this is the most effective format to do it in.

Strategy #33
Use Cards or Token Gifts to Improve Work Relationships

There are as many reasons to send a card or give a token gift as there are cautionary tales about why gift giving can backfire. I remember when I stayed at a home in Bombay, India for a couple of days when I was doing research for my first book. In America, it is customary to bring a gift to someone's home when you are a guest. But when I was leaving my hostess' home on the last day of my visit in Bombay, instead I was given several token gifts as a way of thanking me for honoring them by being their guest. A very different custom than what I was used to, and I cherished those gifts as well as the sentiment.

When you cannot give a gift because there are rules against accepting a gift, which could lead to accusations of influence peddling—whether for a government agency or a specific company with rules against accepting gifts of any value, however small—consider sending a thoughtful greeting card instead.

But if a gift is permissible, especially a token gift with a value of $25 or less, consider sending a gift at the holidays or for a special anniversary, such as to someone who you know has been working for a certain number of years at a company, or for achieving something special, such as landing an especially big deal (but *not* with you or your company which could be misconstrued). If you are unsure about what the rules are at your company about gift giving or receiving, or the economic limits that are recommended, check with your human resource department; if you do not have one, you could ask your co-workers or your supervisor for guidance. Some companies have a limit of $50 to $100 for gifts to those at an executive level. Some companies who exchange gifts among themselves at the holidays suggest keeping the price of the gift as low as $10 or less.

Sending a gift can be a gesture that is positive and sincere and one that has numerous emotional and strategic benefits. But it can sometimes backfire as well. Augusta Nash shared with me about a boss who liked to give her gifts and how embarrassed it made her feel. Says Nash: "I had a boss for five years who showered me with gifts and I always felt uncomfortable because I didn't know what she wanted from it. She gave me a vacuum cleaner. She gave me frequent flyers miles. She sent food over all the time. She gave me little things. She let me borrow her car and she had a very expensive car. It was way overboard and it was all the time. Did I have to work harder? Did I have to be her best friend? What was she buying?"

Nash explains that the situation got worse as the excessive gift giving led to unrealistic expectations about their work relationship: "She wanted to come over to my house when I was having a pot luck dinner with my peers, my colleagues. She got offended because I didn't invite her even though she was at a much higher level than we were. She pouted."

What was the outcome? Nash shared with me that she was grateful that she got a better offer so she was able to leave on her own terms, putting that job and the uncomfortable situation with her boss behind her.

We have all heard that expression, "it's the thought that counts" yet when it comes to gift-giving, the cost of the gift definitely needs to be considered. Sending a gift that is too costly can actually be more offensive to the recipient than sending something that is too cheap, which reflects badly on the gift giver's taste. Most government agencies have rules or laws against gift giving even at the holiday time. In the private sector, it is much more a question of what is the standard for that industry as well as for a particular company. If you are in negotiation with an individual or company, it might be advised to avoid gift giving at least till after the deal is finalized-signed, sealed, and delivered.

If appropriate and permissible, giving gifts in business can be a very joyful and positive way of communicating appreciation for an employee, client, customer, coworker, or service provider. When I was interviewing men and women for my book, *Making Your Office Work for You*, I remember noticing a very attractive business card holder on the desk of an executive at a major Manhattan firm. She told me, with pride, that her secretary had given that to her for the holidays. I recall an interview I did with the owner of an employment agency. In one part of her oversized office, there was a box that was almost as big as half of her impressive office space. In that box were dozens of baskets with goodies for the holidays. Those baskets were going to be mailed out to her top clients as a way of saying "thanks" at the holiday time. When I attend the Frankfurt Book Fair, there are many gift exchanges between agents and publishers, or publishers and publishers. The gifts are usually not very expensive, and often it is a token gift that is native to their country, such as a handmade bookmark from Indonesia or note paper from Korea, but it is a ritual that is as much a part of the business meeting as exchanging business cards or discussing the latest projects that are available.

Even in these economically-challenged times, gift giving is a way of honoring a workplace or business relationship. Sometimes it will be expressed by making a donation to a charity in the name of another company or even an individual in lieu of a personal gift.

It is very important that the gift is appropriate and that it moves the relationship along in a positive way rather than backfiring. Here are some questions to ask yourself before you buy a gift for someone at work or in business:

- Is it acceptable at this company, association, or agency to send a gift?
- Are there any financial guidelines on how much I can spend?
- Is the gift I plan to buy appropriate in a business situation, not too personal an item?
- Do I have the correct address or a home address to send the gift to in case it is a perishable item and someone might be away for the holidays?
- Will I feel awkward if the person I am sending the gift to decides to reciprocate and send me a gift in return?
- Am I sending this gift because of a heartfelt positive feeling, such as someone achieving a goal, having a baby, celebrating the closing of a deal, etc., or is it to try to ingratiate myself to this person?

When appropriate and not taken to extremes, gift giving can be a useful way to strengthen or improve a workplace or business relationship but the relationship has to be there and the gift has to be appropriate to that relationship. It should not be so out of place or inappropriate that the recipient, like Nash, as noted above, has an uncomfortable feeling of, "What does my boss want from me?" or "What is my colleague's hidden agenda behind this gift?"

But what if you, unlike Nash, cannot leave your job, or you do not want to end a client or customer relationship, and you have a gift giving (or receiving) situation that is uncomfortable? What are some ways you could handle it without jeopardizing your work relationship?

Gift From a Coworker
- Decline the gift politely. "I'm sorry I can't accept this. It's too much. I feel uncomfortable." Return it and let your coworker decide what to do about it.
- Ask what it's for. "Why are you giving me this gift?" Based on the answer, decide what you will do.

Gift From a Boss
- Say "Thanks, but I feel uncomfortable accepting this."
- Respond with, "It's too much for me to feel comfortable accepting."
- Again, ask what it's for. If it is in lieu of a bonus and if it is, you could see if you could exchange it for the cash value of the gift.

Gift From a Client or Customer
- If it's a gift that is within acceptable financial guidelines but the item makes you uncomfortable, such as jewelry or a personal item that might imply an ulterior motive, you can either return the item or just dispose of it without making a fuss.
- If you have a policy against it, you can thank them and then let them know that you are donating it.

Chapter Six

⬤ ⬤ ⬤

Coping With a Range
of Workplace Situations

Strategy #34
Bridge the Generations

I *asked a 31-year-old CEO* who has a Silicon Valley, California-based IT company with six others if he finds there are generational issues that he has to deal with at his company. Does he find it challenging to work with those older or younger? The gist of his reply was that it wasn't a problem because "I only hire other 31-year olds."

His bluntness highlights the growing challenge of intergenerational issues in the workplace and in business in general. Besides the issue of older workers remaining, or returning, to the workplace, often finding themselves working for bosses half their age, intergenerational issues include younger persons entering the workforce for the first time with an unrealistic sense of entitlement (e.g., about salaries, how long it is going to take to get ahead, and what hours they are expected to work), as well as some of the middle-aged workers who feel little allegiance to their current employer whom they fear will pink-slip them at the drop of a hat. These seasoned workers seem to have more loyalty to the headhunters or online search job engines that they search daily, or to their school or college alumni, or to former coworkers or bosses, than to the company who is providing them with a paycheck but no job security.

We now have at least four generations in the workplace:

- Traditionalists/The Greatest Generation (those born before 1946)
- Baby Boomers or Boomers (those born between 1946 and 1966)
- Generation X (those born between 1967 and 1981)
- Generation Y/Millennials (those born between 1982 and 2002) (also known as EchoBoomers, or the children of Baby Boomers)

What are some of the key distinctions in the way each generation approaches work and the workplace? The statements that follow are, of course, stereotypes and there is certainly room for individual differences within each type. But the common cultural, technological and social factors that each generation lived through does shape that generation. That, in turn, impacts on what expectations members of that generation bring to the workplace as well as how they deal with the workplace and their business relationships.

The Traditionalists or The Greatest Generation lived through the two defining events: the Great Depression of the 1930s, and World War II. They have known sacrifice, postponing dreams and goals, enduring financial hardships, as well as working in a country with more widespread military commitments. A late retirement to a sunny climate to golf and relax was the goal for most in this age group until the economic downtown of 2008 forced some of the Traditionalists back into the workforce.

The Baby Boomers (or Boomers) grew up in the shadow of World War II with the 60s and Women's Lib as two of their defining events. Moving out from the city into the suburbs and providing their children with a good education were the goals for many of these Baby Boomers as parents. Boomers are determined to do things differently than their parents, including their approach to retirement. However, with the economic crisis of 2008, even those who planned to retire in their late fifties to early sixties were finding themselves pushed back into the workforce to replenish their retirement funds or just to survive economically.

Generation X is the generation that grew up with technology as a comfortable, acceptable way to communicate and interact. President Barack Obama, while technically one of the younger Boomers, born in 1961, appealed to Generation X and younger voters because he was perceived to be one of them. One of the hallmarks of President Obama's presidential campaign was how comfortable he was using technology to communicate with his supporters, including his active participation on Twitter.com, as well as his own admission of how pivotal his Blackberry was to his ability to communicate with his close circle of friends.

Generation Y or the Millennials are the youngest ones in today's workforce, ranging in age from 18 to 25. Those in Generation Y, even more than Generation Xers, grew up with technology as an expected and predictable part of their lives. Cell phones and the Internet are completely natural for this age group. In general, they also expect everything to happen very quickly and are much more likely to be comfortable multitasking than any of the previous generations.

Bruce Tulgan, who has spent the last two decades studying the difference in generations in the workplace, and whose most recent book is called *Not Everybody Gets a Trophy: How to Manage Generation Y*, points out some of the work traits of the younger generation. Says Tulgan: "They're likely to show up on the first day, filled with energy and enthusiasm. 'I'm here. I've been to your website. There are seventeen things we should change about your company right now.' The person who is greeting him says, 'Golly. You've been here for five minutes. My first day, I kept my mouth shut and kept my head down and you show up on your first day and you tell me how you're going to change the business.'"

Even younger new hires may have a more dramatic clash at work when, as Tulgan notes, they say to their new manager, "'I can't come in by nine. I need to have Thursdays off. Any chance I can work from home?'"

Another challenge today that Tulgan sees is that the younger and less experienced workers tend to tire quickly with a task. As Tulgan notes: "They want to do something new. 'Gosh, I've been doing this for weeks and weeks so I don't want to do it anymore.'" The manager's attitude is, "Now that you know how to do it, we want you to do it. You're good at it so you can keep doing it." But the younger worker thinks, "Now that I know how to do it, I want to do something new."

Bridging generational divides can also mean that the older generation has to be more patient with the younger ones. If you do not let the younger, less experienced workers learn how to do a task but instead you do it for them, the company, in the long run, will suffer. In the short run, it will undermine the younger person's confidence. Trainer Augusta Nash shares a situation that occurred in her office that supports that perspective: "I told my administrative assistant to create a document for me, explained the conditions of satisfaction to her, and went my merry way. But the next afternoon, since she had not yet completed the document, even though the deadline wasn't up, I sat down and created it myself, asked her to make copies for me, and I bopped out of my office. She seemed upset but I didn't take the time to ask her why. Later that day, as I was driving back from an appointment, I realized I had undermined her authority and her motivation by the way I had handled the situation. I went back into the office, walked up to her desk, and apologized. I told her I was feeling nervous about getting the document done so I did it myself and didn't bother to let her know what was going on [with] me. And I was very sorry. She burst into tears and said how she thought she had let me down, etcetera, etcetera. I reinforced that it was all about me. After that experience, she worked even harder for me and I communicated more with her. We had become a team!"

Joyce Gioia shares how she deals with generational issues especially related to tattoos and dress: "Employers and corporate leaders who are upset by these tattoos and body armor just need to 'get over it'. This warning is actually a message to all of us, because sometimes it's hard for me. I've been really turned off by tattoos and body piercings We all need to get over it, because within reason, this is just how these young people express themselves."

Based on my own experiences as well as my research, here are some additional tips for working across the generations:

1. Know the broad characteristics for each generation, such as the Baby Boomers who matured during the 60s when peace and love were valued and making lots of money was not emphasized as much as joining the Peace Corps and changing the world. However, remember there are still very strong individual differences within each generational stereotype. For example, there are upper middle class Baby Boomers who have become millionaires and even billionaires who very much value money and there are scores of others who are struggling just to get by not because they are magnanimous do-gooders but they have fallen on hard times and are broke.

2. If you find it hard to work with those in other age groups because of how they dress, behave, talk, or even their approach to work and work relationships, take a workshop on generational issues or hire a coach specializing in helping individuals to overcome those emotional or professional obstacles. It is up to you to adapt to the intergenerational workplace rather than expect it to cater to you.

3. Emphasize what is similar among the generations rather than different. Maybe the Millennials are more comfortable texting or instant messaging a communication than picking up the phone, but being honest, prepared, and on

time are standards that cut across the generations.

4. Deemphasize your age. You do not have to lie about it but you can focus on your experience, if you are older, rather than a number or, if you are younger, highlight your enthusiasm, energy, and that your training is more recent and "cutting edge."

5. Work out some scenarios in your head for any of the standard questions you might be asked. I recall a talk show that called me about half a dozen years ago. They were considering me as an expert on one of their upcoming shows. The booker asked me how old I was. I was completely flabbergasted. No show had ever asked me that before. I was, after all, being considered as an expert, not someone in the audience. I blurted out my age; the interviewer immediately lost interest in me. When I shared what happened with a friend over coffee who was a generation younger than me, she suggested that I should have said something like this, "Twenty. That's the number of years that I've spent becoming an expert in this field. That's the only number that you should be concerned with." Another approach could have been/could be to turn the question around and instead ask, "Why do you want to know?" If someone shares with you what reason they have for gathering that information, you are in a better position to decide whether or not you want to share that fact with them.

6. What we're talking about is that there are different ways of communicating. A Traditionalist might write a thank you note, while a Boomer might e-mail you. A GenX might text you and a Millennial doesn't know at all that you're supposed to express thanks. Look at that and what it means.

7. The different groups learn differently. The Boomers and the Traditionalists learn through writing and having

mentors and seeing how it's done. The Xers and the Millenials learn through simulation and role playing, training, and games. If you are trying to reach them, use a simulation.

8. There may be a fear of new technology for the Traditionalists and some Boomers. You can encourage the Gen X and Millennials, who are technology-savvy, to assist the others, and in exchange the older folks can assist them with networking skills, meeting and greeting. You can have a combination.

9. Some of the younger generation Millennials are resentful that they're only called in for technology and not their opinions. They are impatient and want a career map. The concept of loyalty to an organization isn't their orientation but you can argue that organizations have let them down. Make sure they have portable skills and they can work anywhere.

10. Many Traditionalists will preface anecdotes with "In my day…" but that turns off the younger generation.

11. To older generations, wearing tattoos meant you were in the Navy or in prison. For some of the younger generations, it's a symbol of expression.

12. Millennials will talk to you. Millennials want feedback right away. For the older generations, the attitude about the performance review is that no news is good news.

13. The younger generation has a different attitude toward seniority and advancement. "I don't need to be here that long" or "I shouldn't be there that long."

If someone does not feel comfortable in a particular generation, they may be seen as a "cusper" who could identity strongly with one or the other generation.

Fortunately not all younger people consider working with older people something to be avoided. Dr. Wright, a 37-year-old

California-based TV producer and host who has her own cable show on entrepreneurship, welcomes the possibility of working with a range of ages. As she said in our interview: "Working with sixty-year-olds? For me, it's an exciting opportunity. Working with a person who's older gives me the opportunity for a different perspective. I only see things the way I see them. It's always good for me to look at things historically. 'Hey, we've had this recession before, yes, we can make it through this. We can be okay,' makes it a lot more palatable. I also like working with younger people because they will push things and let you know this is how they're doing it."

Strategy #35
Manage Gender Differences

These days you're likely to find an equal number of men and women in the workplace at different levels. If you're a man, there's a greater chance that your boss is going to be a woman than ever before. If you're a woman, you're more likely to work for a woman and how you relate to a woman as a boss is going to be more of an issue than it might have been in the past.

The strategy is to strive to avoid distinguishing between people's genders. Your primary relationship with them is that of a coworker or a boss and whether they're one sex or the other shouldn't matter. If you have trouble avoiding gender as an issue, it could make the work environment uncomfortable. She's your boss first, she's a woman second. Try harder to get beyond gender; if you need help with this, seek out a coach or therapist with whom you can explore the roots of your work relationships. What emotional triggers might be causing this? Try to eliminate in your mind as much as possible the sexual differences because that can cause problems.

If a business situation or conversation becomes even remotely sexual, flirtatious, or takes on a different tone, that's when trouble starts. If you're a woman, you are not going to want to dress provocatively because that is going to make it harder for your male coworkers or boss to treat you as a non-sexual being. Sadly, there are still people who hold their gender prejudices dearly. For example, in a recent *New York Times* article, Carol Smith, senior vice president and chief brand officer at a media company, was quoted as saying: "In my experience, female bosses tend to be better managers, better advisers, mentors, rational thinkers. Men love to hear themselves talk. I'm so generalizing. I know I am. But in a couple of places I've worked, I would often say, 'Call me in 15 minutes after the meeting starts and then I'll come,' because I will have missed all the football. I will have missed all the 'what I did on the golf course.' I will miss the four jokes, and I can get into the meeting when it's starting."

If someone were to ask you the question that the *New York Times* asked of Carol Smith: "It sounds as if you've thought a lot about men versus women as managers," what would *your* answer be? If your answer reflects some preconceived notions or prejudices, assess where those judgments have come from and how those views might be hampering your work relationships.

What about gender differences in phone calls as well as written communications? Have you noticed any disparities? Do you find men in authority can be blunt, to a fault? Or that women tend to include more personal information and to write longer e-mails than males? Or are these just gender stereotypes that do not ring true for you?

Strategy #36
Sort Out the Challenges of Working With a Friend

Just because you and your friends work together does not mean either the business or the friendship are doomed. Amie Garcia is a California-based businesswoman who, along with two of her closest friends, has been a co-partner in running a shoe company for babies and toddlers since 2005. Their positive business experience defies the cliché about *never* working for or with a friend. The three women are all married and they each have two young children. As working moms, they founded the business to enable them to have more control over their time, so they could be their own bosses while still prioritizing their families. Amie lives in San Diego, Mitzi in San Francisco, and Laura in Washington, D.C. Laura is the only one who has another job in addition to being part of the company and raising her children.

Amie, who previously worked as an elementary school teacher and assistant principal, explains: "Trust has always played an important part in all of my work relationships. As a teacher and assistant principal, I felt that trust was the foundation to build strong relationships with families and gaining respect as an administrator. As a small business owner, I share a business that I started with my two close friends, Laura and Mitzi, that I trust one hundred percent. Laura and Mitzi have been friends since college. Mitzi and I met when we were pregnant for the first time. I then met Laura through Mitzi."

What are other secrets to their success? They also have specialized roles helping to reduce the potential that competitiveness could negatively impact on their ability to keep their company running smoothly. Amie says: "Each of us are involved in all aspects of the business but over time we've also created roles for ourselves, based on what we love. Mitzi's love is designing, my love is overseeing manufacturing and finding sustainable materials, Laura handles our online store and oversees our charity program. (We donate ten percent of our monthly sales to rotating charities)."

Instead of potentially being in competition with each other if, let's say, they were all trying to generate sales or do the design work, they have divided up the job functions to run the company and each has one or two areas with little overlap. Amie handles manufacturing as well as the accounting. Laura handles direct sales and the website. Mitzi handles design. Mitzi also thinks that their company works because they share a similar positive feeling about their company. Says Mitzi: "I feel so passionate about what I do that it has sort of inflamed the business and we all feel that way. I couldn't be in business with some of my dearest friends. It's because we're so similar and we're all designers so it might be hard to run a business together. The beauty [of our company] is when you talk to each of us, we have very different personalities. We each have two children but we all share this one other child and that's our business. We run our business the way we run our lives. We're working at our dream job. We give ten percent of our proceeds to charity. We do fabulous things for our community. Our work is a reflection of how we live our lives."

For others, like CEO Richard Laermer, who is an author and who also has his own public relations company, working with old friends did not work out for him but he has found that he has become friends with some of his employees when the friendship naturally evolved through their shared work experiences.

The former director at a financial services company shares about one of the three friendships that developed out of the thirty employees who reported to him: "I knew Craig and his work and when I was setting up the new division and he wasn't working, I asked him if he would be interested in coming on as a consultant. That led to him working for me for the next seven years, and a friendship developed during that period."

The job ended eight years ago, but, "We remained friends" he explains.

Take the following self-quiz to help you decide if you could work for or with a particular friend:

SELF-QUIZ: WORKING FOR OR WITH A FRIEND

1. Have you picked the friend with whom you wish to work very carefully? Not all friendships, or business situations, are equal.

2. Do you and this friend share the same values, such as honesty, loyalty, trust, a similar work ethic, or family priorities?

3. Is there a way to divide the responsibilities so that you are in complementary rather than competitive roles?

4. If you will be reporting to your friend, are you able to take orders from your friend, separating the friendship from her supervisory role?

5. If your friend will report to you, are you able to do the same?

6. Are you able to be objective at work or in your business despite your emotional attachment to your friend?

7. If the arrangement does not work out, are you or your friend prepared to leave the job?

8. If you are not at the same level, are you still able to work well together despite your different status or roles?

9. If you are in business together, even though you are friends, do you have a legal document that you are relying on as well as an exit strategy for the business if the arrangement does not work out?

10. Are you willing to make a choice if you have to between saving your job and saving your friendship?

If you answered "yes" to all ten questions, working with or for your friend has a better chance of a positive outcome. If you answered "no" to one or more questions, you should seriously reconsider if this is an arrangement that is in your best interest. If you answered "no" to three or more questions, especially to question 10, "Are you willing to make a choice if you have to between saving your job or saving your friendship?" you may be better off having a "no friends" policy at work or in business that you strictly enforce.

Unlike Amie, Mitzi, and Laura's positive partnership business experience, described earlier in this chapter, some businesses that are co-owned by friends do not fare as well. Then what should you do? Forty-one-year-old Bill and his partner ran their advertising agency for seven years but they were more than partners. They had become best friends. Bill married and became a parent during the years that he and Steve ran the company together. Then Steve began a relationship with Bill's new assistant, Lisa. There were rumors that they were dating but Bill didn't think anything of it. However, within months, Steve announced that he was leaving the company and that Bill's assistant was coming with him. Steve started a rival company using money from Lisa's inheritance (Lisa would own a 51% stake in the new company.)

I interviewed Bill two years after this happened, and he was still in shock. He's still trying to figure out what to do about what happened. Steve still owns one third of Bill's company even though Bill has technically bought him out. He's considered suing but he doesn't know if the money, expense, and trauma of a law suit would be worth it in the long run. "Why didn't I see this coming?" Bill asks.

What did Bill learn from dealing with this difficult situation? Bill replies: "I certainly learned never to have another partner and never to be so open and trusting again. Now I keep my work relationships separate from my personal relationships."

We have seen the positive example of Amie, Mitzi, and Laura, who were all close friends when they became partners who are managing a children's shoe manufacturing company. So far, their partnership is going fine. So eliminating partnerships because something might sour down the road is not the answer. Being more aware of the warning signs that the partnership is changing and no longer is working a better strategy.

Here are some of the warning signs to heed:

- You used to have very open communication at work but your partner is becoming more secretive.

- You spend less time together outside of work.
- The work has become much more disproportionate but the terms of the partnership have not shifted to reflect that change.
- You have a feeling in your gut that your partner is planning something but you do not know exactly what that could be.

Strategy #37
How to End a Business Relationship With a Friend

Have you ever had a business relationship with someone that you thought was a friend and then had to sever your business relationship? How did it impact on the friendship? That's a very challenging situation and one that is hard to have a positive outcome. A coach and speaker shared with me that he had used his friend for many years as the accountant for his business. However, he decided he no longer wanted to use him as an accountant. Much to his surprise, his friend said to him that he could not be his friend if he was no longer his accountant.

Sadly, that is too often the outcome when friends do business together and one or both friends end the work situation. However, there may be a way to increase the likelihood that the friendship *will* survive. Here are some suggestions:

- If you have to end your working relationship with a friend, or someone who has become a friend through work, tell them over the phone or in person. Avoid letting them know in an e-mail or a letter especially in a form letter or e-mail that is going out to others with whom you have to end your work relationship. This relationship is unique because it is a friendship and not just a work relationship. It needs to be handled with much more sensitivity as well as through a personal connection.

- Emphasize that your friendship and its continuation are very important to you.

- Without lying or exaggerating, if it is indeed circumstances beyond your control, let your friend know that the difficult decision was someone else's or, if it was yours alone, that it was based on something that should not be interpreted as reflecting on your friend's work or competence.

- Most important of all, be understanding if your friend's feelings are hurt. Let him or her express that upset and sadness and don't be shocked or pushed away by those reactions. If someone is super sensitive, it will be harder to take the rejection than for others. Some will take it in stride and say, "that's business," and not let it impact on your friendship whatsoever.

- Give your friend time to get over what happened and, as soon as it seems comfortable, get together again for coffee, dinner, or a movie out, reestablishing this new post-working together phrase in your friendship.

Strategy #38
Office Romances

A book on work relationships would not be complete without a discussion of the pros and cons of office romance and how to deal with it whether you are the one considering such an arrangement or you are watching coworkers or a boss and a subordinate as their office romance blossoms (or backfires).

The key considerations about office romance are:

- Are the individuals who are involved in the romance at the same level, e.g., coworkers, or is it a supervisor/subordinate situation?

- Are those involved in the romance single and available or are one or both parties involved with someone or married with children and this relationship, for starters, is an affair?
- Did the individuals start working together as an involved couple or did their romance evolve after they began work?

If the individuals who are involved in the romance are at the same level, such as two coworkers, there is usually less of a problem, especially if the romance peters out, than if the romance involves a superior who has a subordinate reporting to him or her. With the heightened awareness about allegations of sexual harassment, it is key that anyone who wants to begin a romantic relationship with someone who is a subordinate consider the potential consequences of such a relationship very carefully. If the other person wants to date, there could be no harm in asking. But if the feelings are not returned, the employee who is courted by the superior could see it as evidence of sexual harassment and it could lead to reprimands or worse by the human resource department whether or not a formal complaint is lodged.

Even if the developing romance is between equals, such as coworkers, it is key that both weigh the potential consequences of their shift from a coworker to coworker + romantic involvement relationship if the romance part of the relationship does not work out. Over the years, when I have interviewed managers about this issue, the consensus was that as long as the employees were at the same level, the relationship was consensual, and there was no diminution in productivity because of the romantic relationship, it was okay. But one or both coworkers should think about what they would do if the relationship faded, and working nearby or even at the same company became emotionally too stressful. Who would leave? Who would stay? How would they handle the potential jealousy of other coworkers?

There are some basic "rules" relating to office romance

whether the relationship is between equals or those of disparate status:

- Avoid touching each other in an intimate way in front of other coworkers, employees, or bosses.
- Avoid using nicknames or romantic labels, such as "Dear," "Darling," "Sweetheart," or "Sugar" in front of others.
- Keep the details of your intimate relationship to yourselves.
- Don't flaunt your intimacy.
- If there is a workplace romance policy, find out what it is. If it is necessary to clear your intentions with management or human resources, do so.
- If a contract is required for executives who have office romances, find out the details. See if you want your own lawyer to review the contract before you and your romantic partner sign it.

If you decide to work together and you are already romantically involved, if there are other employees at your company—it is more than just a husband and wife two-person firm—the same "rules" would apply when you're around others, such as avoiding using terms that might make others uncomfortable, or touching each other in a way that would not be appropriate in the workplace. If you start off working together as a couple who is romantically involved, however, it will obviously be less jarring to fellow employees or management than if the romantic relationship occurs after you start the job.

Yes, love is an emotion that many will attest to its power when the chemistry is there and the basic instincts take hold. But if an office relationship has not yet become a romance, there are ways to head off the escalating situation so it does not become inevitable that the attraction will lead to an affair or a romance.

The term "office spouse" has become quite common to describe this phenomenon: this is an office relationship that is pre-romantic but it is definitely heading in that direction. How is it possible to diminish the increasing attraction at work if one or both parties would prefer *not* to get romantically involved? Short of having someone transferred, or leaving the job yourself, what could someone do? Minimizing or eliminating time alone is an obvious start. It's a no brainer that you want to avoid taking business trips together, even if you have separate hotel rooms, or working late into the night when it's just the two of you at the office. More subtle but still a trap to avoid is badmouthing your spouse or romantic partner, who is not around to defend himself or herself, putting the office "mate" in the position of becoming a confidante, the "you and me against the world" phenomena where you start to feel as if you are the only ones who understand each other.

Strategy #39
Working With a Family Member or Romantic Partner

This is different from the previous strategy, which deals with handling office romance challenges as they arise at work. This strategy offers advice about dealing with issues that may develop because you are working for or with a family member or a romantic partner. For some men and women, working for a parent or a sibling may be the perfect situation. There is more job security than in most companies where you can be fired at will. It's a lot harder to fire your son or your wife. You also can know more about the boss than if you walk into a job interview basically having googled the company president and just read up a few articles about him or her. You really know this person because you've been family members since birth or through marriage.

For some romantic couples, whether married, engaged, living

together, or dating, working together can be the best of both worlds. They get to earn a living and they also get to spend time together during the day, not just in the evenings when they might be tired or, if they have children or even a second job, it is hard to find time for each other. By working together, they also have a work connection that can help their relationship to be stronger than if they are so removed from what each one does during the day that they have less and less in common.

Beverly Solomon is married to Pablo Solomon, an artist whose work has been sold internationally. For the last five years, Beverly has also run Pablo's art career. Working together suits this couple. As Beverly explains: "I am the full-time muse and business manager for my husband Pablo Solomon, an internationally recognized artist. We have seriously worked together on his art career for about five years now. The hardest part in the beginning was defining work boundaries. In other words, who was responsible for what and then leave that person alone to do their job. Being a husband/wife team, that was the most sensitive area to deal with. We enjoy living and working together in a beautiful setting but we can feel isolated at times."

Fifty-two-year-old Caroline runs a media company in Georgia which her parents founded. Her father passed away and her mother's health has been poor so she tried to pass the company reins along to Caroline but, as we will see, the transfer of authority has not been complete. As Caroline notes: "When my mother had a heart attack and almost died, she made me president of the company. But that was on paper only. She runs the company, makes the decisions, etcetera. She will not discuss succession issues at all. Tells me, 'You'll figure it out' when I ask how I'll do the job she does when she (as she puts it) 'shuffles off to Buffalo.' She says talking about it will make it happen sooner. (I'm an existentialist so I'm not buying into that one.)"

What could Caroline do to help the situation along now that her mother is back at the top? Offering her mother specific job functions that keep her occupied but give Caroline the final say as well as overreaching decision-making authority is one possibility. Her mother, for example, could be in charge of setting up meetings with local media and communicating with previous clients to see if there is a way to jump start new projects and business with them.

If this mother and daughter team did not have a positive relationship outside of work, her mother might be trying to keep control of the company as a way to have something to talk to Caroline about. Caroline could start setting up a weekly dinner meeting with her mother and maybe even going to a movie every now and then. That might help her mother to make a break from needing work as a way of bonding with her daughter.

If her mother is lonely and is returning to run the business out of boredom and loneliness, Caroline could try to get her mother interested in philanthropic work outside of their business which might take her focus off running the business that Caroline wants to run on her own.

If her mother really just wants someone to talk to and she does not have an assistant, getting her one could help her mother to have someone to talk to at work besides Caroline.

Finally, if all else fails, if the funds are there and it would be a good deal, buy a second company and let her mother run that one.

Strategy #40
Contend With Not Getting Paid or Money Challenges

"Someone hired us, used our services, and then demanded a refund," says a 44-year-old entrepreneur. Sound familiar? Who has not been cut out of a payment that he or should have been given? A fee that is not paid if you are a self-employed entrepreneur. A promised bonus that is denied. Sometimes it really is economics—as you find out a month or two after the agreed upon fee fails to arrive, followed by the bankruptcy notices that appear in your in box with the do's and don'ts of collecting your fee and all the red tape involved—that might lead you to decide to just forget about it.

Whether it's four hundred dollars, four thousand, or forty thousand, getting stiffed on payment is a tough reality in the work world that happens too often. The experience can be so powerful that some, such as Michael Hughes, consider "non-payment of services" to be the #1 worst work-related relationship thing that ever happened to him. He says: "It was in the early stages of my business. It was a business transaction between two individuals and [the] two had primarily agreed to bring me on board. I knew both parties. In hindsight I should have known there would have been a problem but chose to overlook it because I needed the money. But it's the only time I haven't been paid for my services. There were some personality issues between he and I that were almost irreconcilable differences. I chose to walk away...[this was] probably the most negative issue I've ever had revolving around a business relationship."

What are some suggestions to avoid failing to get paid in the first place? Obviously this will apply, in general, to independent contractors, entrepreneurs, or freelancers, who work on a project basis, rather than those on a steady salary, but today, especially in the private sector, even with a traditional nine-to-five job a salaried position is not guaranteed. Here are some tips for avoiding nonpayment of your fee especially as it relates to a relationship issue:

- Try to only work with those with whom you have a strong, positive connection.
- Despite the personal connection, however, let whoever owes you the money know that this is a business situation and that you did the work, it was acceptable, and you deserve to be paid.

- If there is a problem on their end in terms of having the funds to pay you, agree to work out a formal payment arrangement, clarified in writing, such as a couple of hundred or a couple of thousand dollars a month, depending upon how much is owed, rather than no payment at all.
- Keep the dialogue open. If possible, have other connections to this one resource so you are more likely to be able to keep track of it even if it relocates to another location or changes its name.

Chapter Seven

● ◆ ●

Improve Workplace
or Business Relationships

Strategy #41
Create a Functional Versus a Dysfunctional Workplace

We've all heard of dysfunctional families. But what about dysfunctional workplaces? You'd recognize one if you saw it. Maybe you have even had the misfortune of working in one. Here's just one example described by a practical nurse-turned-entrepreneur: "I worked in a nursing home for almost four years and you have never seen anything like it! The backstabbing and politics were unbelievable. There [were] these people, supposed to be caring individuals, they can't stand being in a room together. Nobody looks out for anybody, if there is a way to hurt a fellow employee, they will find it. And the residents are not immune either. Some nurses and CNA's [certified nursing assistants] talk to the resident as if their entire reason or life is to make their nurse's life miserable. One of the girl's houses burned to the ground. Would you believe her coworkers called the fire marshal and told him she had set the fire herself?"

Fortunately it is not that way everywhere. She continues: "It is not like this in all facilities, but this one is beyond anything I had ever experienced. And nobody confesses to there being a problem."

What does a functional workplace look like? Here are the positive conditions that you might look for in a work situation, especially if you have a choice among several job opportunities:

- There is consistency between what you are promised and what is delivered. Employees seem happy to be working there.

- In a traditional white collar office setting, your work station, even if it is a chair in shared space, is as ergonomically sound as possible, enabling you to have the best chance of avoiding the physical challenges related to sitting at a computer too long.

- In other work settings, such as a hospital, television studio, schoolroom, the office environment is designed to suit the unique demands of the kind of work that is carried out there.

- Gossip is frowned upon.

- There is a clear division of labor or chain of command so you know who is in charge.

- You have a realistic idea of what you have been hired to do and, if those responsibilities or expectations change in time, you are made aware of those changes.

- You know who will evaluate you, and when, and what they will be looking for in your performance.

- The ambiance or atmosphere is a positive one.

- You look forward to going to work most days and find the time passes quickly.

- There is a trust throughout the work environment (or, if you are self-employed, between you and your client or customers) that you are all performing with each other's best interests in mind.

- If there are any grievances, there is an established way for handling concerns or conflicts.

By contrast, here is a depiction to a toxic workplace:

- Employees tend to "yes" the boss when asked for feedback.

- Working late or weekends is expected and required without additional compensation.
- Favoritism is rampant in hiring and in promotions.
- Innovativeness is discouraged.
- Expectations are unrealistic.
- Job responsibilities are blurred or crossing into too many functions.
- Direct reports have too many bosses with competing demands.
- You find yourself just working till you retire, and that's five years away!
- You are bored.
- You are asked to perform job functions beyond your capabilities and without having the opportunity to get the training that you need.
- Promises are broken by management.
- You can't wait for Friday (TGIF) and you dread going back to work on Monday.
- This job, and the people you work with or for, make you feel bad about yourself.
- There are countless meetings just for the sake of having a meeting.
- Co-workers talk about each other behind their backs.
- Cliques are rampant.
- Human resources reports to your boss so you have no one to complain to if you have justified grievance with your boss.
- Racist or sexist language is heard frequently.
- Ethnic slurs or jokes are made by your coworkers or boss.
- Deadlines are unrealistic and changed often.
- You find yourself thinking about work constantly and it's negatively impacting on your sleep and stress levels.

- Your romantic partner or children rarely get to spend any time with you during the week and you're also working most weekends.
- Everyday you expect someone to tell you that either your job or the company is folding.
- Instead of inspiring by praise and positive examples, employees are bombarded through e-mails that they are not doing enough to try to make the company successful.

If you are stuck working at a toxic workplace, until you are able to move to another job, or until the head of the company who is setting the negative tone has an epiphany and starts behaving in a more positive way, you have to remember that you can only try to work on your own behavior and performance. Write e-mails back to your toxic boss, but try not to send unless you want to get reprimanded or even fired. Also remember that the toxicity might be due to the company having serious financial troubles that you are not privy to; depersonalize the toxicity and negativity as much as possible. If the toxicity persists, it may be time to look for a new job.

If you are in a positive work environment but the company is starting to have financial troubles, or you are not getting along with your boss and it is going to be hard to turn things around, it may be time to look for a new job, in your own time and at your own pace. That way you can leave when it is best for you. Working in a positive work environment is definitely preferred to being in a toxic one, but sometimes that is just not enough to sustain your job or the company.

Strategy #42
Build Trust in the Workplace

Evidence of mistrust in a workplace environment includes the following:

- An employer is so distrustful that his employees will take advantage of him that he wants every employee in full view in the office at all time; he monitors how often anyone takes a bathroom break, however, legitimate those breaks might be.
- A coworker fails to let another employee know about a phone call that she received, whether out of laziness or an unconscious wish to sabotage her associate.

Trust is key to a functional workplace. Where there is a dysfunctional workplace or work relationships, it is usually because trust never existed or it has eroded.

How do you build trust? Here are some of the ways that trust is earned and maintained:

- Information is freely exchanged. Contact details on customers or clients are shared among employees and/or consultants so follow-up is possible whether someone is on vacation or their association with the company ends.
- Live up to your promises. If you say you're going to do something, do it.
- Be consistent.
- Don't play favorites. Make sure bonuses or benefits are earned and not given out based on favoritism.
- If for any reason you cannot do something, because of other priorities or personal concerns, own up to those changes and let others know deadlines have to be adjusted or projects have to be reconsidered or reassigned.
- Take the time to find out what people think of you and your behavior or policies. Cultivate and maintain all levels of relationships, especially by getting together in person.

- Find out what past hurts are being brought into the workplace or into business situations that might poison the water and prevent someone from interacting anew.

Strategy #43
Deal With the Past, Other Relationships, and Value Disparities

THE PAST

Your current workplace or business relationships may not be going as well as you would like your relationships to go because of past mistakes. Of course everyone makes mistakes and it would be nice if those errors in judgment are forgiven and ignored. But someone you work with or for, or even you, may not be starting off on the right foot in completely new situations because past incidents are brought up. For example, a manager did something that showed poor judgment when he was just nineteen and had a drinking problem: he had thrown a bottle at the boss' wife when they were all at an event together. Word got out about that incident and gossip about it has become almost folklore as that incident has haunted and hounded him for decades even though his drinking issues are under control.

Of course no one can undo the past. But if you think there are rumors about you or someone you know that are sabotaging their current reputation, try to get the other person to share those opinions so you can make it clear that those old points of view are outdated and counterproductive to accomplishing the excellent work today that you (or the other person) are capable of achieving.

Certainly avoid being the one who spreads those old negative rumors especially if you have more recent experiences with a particular individual that are positive and exemplary.

Another way the past impacts on your work relationship is how you or your coworkers or boss got along at home or in previous work situations. Those ways of interacting, whether positive or negative, can be repeated in the present; you and your coworkers or bosses have to deal with the consequences of those behaviors. If your boss was raised by authoritarian parents, and he has learned to lead by power, you have to deal with that behavior trait, however annoying it might be. If you were always taking care of your younger siblings, and you find yourself being overly helpful to interns who should be helping you, you need to be aware of the roots of that way of interacting at work that could be holding you back.

OTHER RELATIONSHIPS

We all have relationships or even second or third jobs that we care about and those pulls can be out of responsibility, a sense of duty, necessity, or even vanity. Some companies or agencies do not allow their employees to have second jobs or to moonlight. Others look the other way as long as those other opportunities do not intrude on the primary company or agency getting the employee's best effort and time. Whether an employee has to take care of an aging parent, a sick loved one, or a dependent infant or child, that job has to come first. A sympathetic and empathetic employer will try to grant as much time off as possible to allow any pressing needs to be addressed such as when a dependent child or elderly parent has to go to a physician or hospital and there is no one else to shoulder that responsibility. But if these competing relationships are the focus of your time and energy too often and for too long, it is going to try the patience of your coworkers, who may have to cover for you and do your work when you are busy, or your boss, who may find your productivity is suffering.

You certainly do not want to sneak around, as so many do, trying to fit in a dentist's appointment between lunch and your next appointment or showing up late because you had to take your child to day care again because your romantic partner overslept. Try to be up front with your coworkers or employer about what's going on in your life that might require you to need some extra time here and there. Or call in and let everyone know you're running late or you have something you must do before, during, or after work (that requires that you leave early now and then or on a regular basis). Offer to work from home, or work extra hours at night or on the weekend, to make up for any lost time rather than hoping you "don't get caught."

"ONE WAY" RELATIONSHIPS AND HOW TO TURN THINGS AROUND

You need to be cognizant of who is in your corner, who is out to sabotage you, and everyone in-between—including those who do not know or care about you. If a one-way or a non-relationship involves someone whom you need in your corner, you are going to have to at least try to turn it around.

- Pretending this person likes you or respects you are not a substitute for reality. Face the situation and try to turn it around.
- Think back to when you first met this person, or first interacted. What was it like? If it was ever positive, at what point did it turn around? Can you pinpoint an exact time and date? If you can, what was the cause?
- If it was something that happened that you could apologize for, consider if apologizing is an okay step for legal and other reasons. If it is the correct action to take, try apologizing. See if that helps to turn things around.
- Send a note, a card, or a token gift if your feelings are heartfelt and see if that positive gesture helps to turn things around.

- If turning the relationship around is not possible no matter what strategies you apply, see if you can delegate this relationship to someone else with whom this person does have a better rapport.

PHYSICAL DISTANCE

There are definite ways you can stay connected to individuals and even to your head office if you have to work remotely. Take the time to make those connections, online, over the phone, or in person so you can foster relationships despite your physical distance. Attend conferences where you all are there in person or set up conference calls so your relationships are more than just one-way e-mails.

VALUE DISPARITY

It is rare that anyone gets to work only with those who share their exact values on everything. In your personal life you can pick and choose those with whom you spend time for fun and friendship, while at work and in business you may have to associate with someone whose values contradict yours. The value disparity may be due to cultural or psychological differences or, even if you share the same background, to other peer and social influences. Ask yourself these questions to see if you can get beyond the value disparity or if it is too fundamental to overlook:

- Is the value disparity just a matter of taste and opinion, or is it so fundamental that you are morally repelled by this individual?
- If a family member espoused or demonstrated this divergent value, could you still associate with them?
- Are there values you have that others might find repugnant but they ignore those disparities?

Depending upon what the value disparity is, you will have to decide if you can work together or if you need to get transferred to another department, find another job, or decline working on a specific project.

Strategy #44
Tackle Cultural and International Issues

In this section, my goal is to raise your consciousness about the cultural differences we all need to consider so cultural or international disparities do not undermine our work relationships. Whether it's over the phone, through e-mail, or in person, someone in Chicago, Illinois does not want to alienate someone they are doing business with who happens to be based in Mumbai, India.

Culture includes language, dress, artifacts, values, etiquette, and even what makes someone comfortable when it comes to personal space. There are almost 200 countries in the world and several billion people. Rather than try to accomplish the impossible task of understanding all the potential differences in the various cultures around the world, focus on something that is more manageable: who do you work with and what culture are they from? Take the time to ask them about their culture, exploring what's similar and what's different. If you travel for business, or even if you send an e-mail to someone in another country, try to find out how they view the world so that you can improve the way you do business together.

E-MAIL ISSUES

Unless you see a picture of someone, do not presume the gender of those with whom you are corresponding through e-mail based on name alone. When in doubt, instead of using Mr. or

Ms., which could offend someone if you pick the wrong gender, considering using the person's entire first and last name, without a "Mr." or "Ms." so it could be either gender and you would therefore not give offense. For instance, you could write to "Chris Smith" instead of Mr. or Ms. Smith since "Chris" could be short for Christina (female) or Christopher (male).

How chatty in e-mail communications is standard for this culture? Be aware of what a particular culture finds appropriate in e-mails especially if there are cross-gender restrictions in how men and women communicate with each other. Do not take offense if someone has a different e-mail style based on international differences as well as his or her personality. Just as there are people who are "phone" people and not "e-mail people," there are those who write long and chatty e-mails and those who like to keep it short and focused only on business.

When sending e-mail, be mindful of time zone issues. If you are used to waking up at 4 a.m. to write e-mails, if your e-mails are time stamped, someone in another time zone, for whom it is 12 noon or 9 at night, might consider your working before dawn a bit odd or you might find yourself labeled a workaholic. If that is going to bother you, consider using a delay system for sending your e-mail; you write the e-mail but you are able to program when it is sent at a later time.

PHONE CALLS

In general, if you want to strengthen your international work relationships, get out from under an overreliance on e-mail and pick up the phone! If you are fearful of the cost of calling internationally, there are many options to explore. You can subscribe to skype.com, which enables you to speak internationally for free over the Internet as long as both parties have the service. You can also buy a prepaid calling card so you need not fear a humongous long distance phone bill. Another option is to add on a flat-rate monthly fee for calling internationally that allows you unlimited calls to certain world destinations.

But if you do pick up the phone and call overseas, be aware that there can be language and dialect barriers that make it hard to understand each other. If you find this to be true, and especially if this was a spontaneous rather than a planned and pre-arranged call, consider keeping the conversation short and suggesting that you call back at another time and that you will have an interpreter on the phone next time to help the conversation along. If this is impractical or you think it will cause more problems than it solves, especially if the phone call will deal with confidential or highly sensitive information that should not be shared with a third party, consider reverting back to e-mail communications in lieu of phone calls.

If you are calling a home-based office, you also do not want to call at two in the morning and wake up the household.

Here are some considerations when calling internationally:

- Know what time zone you are calling, what day it is, and what the time difference is. (A useful free website for that information is www.timeanddate.com.)
- Know if you are calling someone in an outside or a home office, or a cell phone that someone will answer wherever they are, or a phone machine or answering service.
- Be aware of the language challenges that might make it difficult to understand you, even if you speak the same language. Pacing may be different as well as accent. Speak slowly and clearly and, if necessary, ask the person you are speaking with to slow down or to repeat what he or she is saying if you are having a hard time understanding.
- If you are planning to speak for more than a couple of minutes, it might be more polite to set up a phone

interview in advance rather than catch someone off guard.

- Video conferencing is a consideration if you are speaking internationally. Of course make sure this option is acceptable with the individual or group you will be speaking with.

VISITING A FOREIGN WORK RELATIONSHIP

Nothing is as flattering to a work relationship as you taking the time and spending the money to travel to their home country to see their office and their business in its local situation. Those trips, however long or expensive, can help forge business bonds that will last years or decades. (Of course if it does not go well, it can also deepen the rifts and make it even harder to turn the situation around since so much time and effort did go into the trip.)

But you can help along that international business trip if you take into account some situations from the point of view of the business associate you are visiting. For example, make sure your trip is convenient for everyone, not just your business or professional schedule. If you show up in Italy or France in August, don't be personally offended if your business associates, who are on vacation, are either away or refuse to meet with you. In Italy, France, and other countries in Europe where a four-, six- or eight-week long vacation is mandated for those even in an entry level job right out of college, except for a crisis of monumental proportions, that vacation time is sacrosanct.

Internationally, the holiday or vacation times are taken very seriously and visits from foreign work relationships during that time, unless you are a close or best friend, and not just a casual one, will often backfire.

Keep your expectations low even if you have traveled around the world to meet with your business associates. It may be a much bigger deal to you, who made the trip, than it is to those you are visiting, who live there and take their work situation and country for granted.

DRESS

This was a long time ago, I do admit, and I do not know if it would be true in India today, but when I arrived in New Delhi and soon afterwards went on the back of a motorcycle of the translator who accompanied me to a rural area so I could do interviews, men threw stones at me because I was wearing a mini-skirt. You did not show that much leg in India in those days. I realized the error of my ways, started wearing a sari and dressed that way for the rest of my trip, and also avoided walking alone in the towns or cities, and the rest of the trip was without a similar incident.

Back then, I had failed to do my homework about what would be appropriate dress for me during my one-month business trip. I had spent months researching who I should set up meetings with as well as my itinerary as to where I would travel, but I did not consider what to wear. It was a lesson that stayed with me whenever I went on business trips in the future.

In the United States, some offices have become more casual; business casual is Monday through Friday, not just Fridays as it was in the more formal office of the 1980s. Joyce Gioia of The Herman Group, who travels often to Singapore to lead seminars, reminded me that being able to wear jeans to work is still a luxury in some parts of the world: "I was just in Singapore a few months ago and I know that they collect money for charity—five dollars—from people so they can wear blue jeans. For them, it's a real treat."

Of course there are offices in the United States that would consider jeans worn by females or males inappropriate; whereas some workplaces, especially in the film or art professions, would think nothing of a CEO in a sports jacket, shirt, and jeans. When you travel internationally for business, you want to find out what dress is considered appropriate for you for your work-related meetings. You also want to consider the climate differences: June in Australia is considered their winter so you would want to wear a wool suit for a business meeting rather than white cotton pants.

LANGUAGE AND GESTURES

You can't assume that everyone is going to speak English when you travel internationally, especially outside of the major cities. In countries where English is spoken, there are also accents and pacing issues that might make it challenging to understand someone's speech even if it is the same language.

Chanden Tolaney is a New York City-based businessman who grew up in India and moved to the United States when he was 21 years old to attend graduate school in Florida. His business is called culturalelements.com; it is home décor and accessories business inspired by different cultures. Chanden points out that many Americans are unaware that there are 28 states in India and each state has its own regional language and dialect. Says Chanden, "Every state within India has its own sub-language, its own food styles, its own interpretation of religion. There is so much diversity between each state that the accent that someone has varies a lot derived from which state they are from." India has distinct dialects especially different for those who are from North (New Delhi) versus South (Hyderbad) India just as there are dramatic differences in speech and accent in the United States for those who are from the South (Georgia), the North (Brooklyn, New York), or the West (Texas). Yet many lump all Indians together when they consider whether they understand someone who lives in India, or moved to the United States from India.

Of course it is flattering if you learn some expressions when you are visiting an area where little or no English is spoken. When American companies bring executives or other employees to another country to live, they will usually teach them the language before or immediately arriving in that country. It is usually a very intense course but it teaches the basics. Not everyone has the time, resources, or the language ability to master another language or two. Sometimes it's adequate just to learn a few choice words, such as "Please," "Thank you," "My name is——. What is your name?" "Hello" "Good bye." Certainly you can learn just those words even if you need to get an electronic translator to have available, or you could buy a dictionary in the particular language that you will be speaking. You could also look up those words on the Internet and use the free translation services that are readily available.

Mark Jackson, an Alabama-based businessman who started an international conference call service, shared with me how important it is to be up on gesture differences when you are in an international meeting. He was in Brazil for a business meeting and, as Jackson explains, "No one told me that you don't give the 'okay' sign. That basically means the same thing as the middle finger in the United States. I learned that the hard way. A Portuguese interpreter kicked me [and said] 'That does not mean here in Brazil what it means there.' That's not a good thing when you're across from someone and it comes up, 'Would it be all right with your firm if you delayed three weeks?'"

In the United Kingdom, Jackson also learned that if you are in a business meeting or a business lunch, you never take your cell phone and lay it on the table. That is considered rude and insulting because you want the person you are meeting with to think that they have your undivided attention. Says Jackson," If you have your cell phone on the table, that tells that person across the table that you're waiting for someone better to call you."

ATTITUDE TOWARD TIME

When I was in the Fiji airport for six hours, on my way back to the United States from New Zealand, I asked someone about the attitude toward time in Fiji. Her reply was, "Fiji time is no time. You can't be in a rush in Fiji."

Perceptions of time, and how fast things should go in business and work relationships, are very much a cultural phenomenon. This truism was reinforced for Sanjay Burman, a Canadian-based publisher of motivational books who went to India in the summer of 2008 to try to make a deal to bring a couple of authors to North America. Burman explains: "What killed the deal is that I wanted to work around the clock to get the deal done, and Indian culture, like European culture, you don't go to meetings till one in the afternoon. 'I'll get you the documents in a while' turns into two, three days and that upset me and I got edgy. So we didn't get the deal accomplished."

Burman regretted the way he behaved because it killed the deal. "It's one of those things—they really do work to live, and we live to work," he says.

It was a lesson that he took to heart, adding, "If you can put yourself in that mentality, you will get a lot more accomplished, plus you will lead a happier life."

Different cultures have varied standards about what is late. In America, we like people to show up right on time or it's considered rude. But in Columbia, Latin America, you could be fifteen minutes late and it would be considered acceptable. Yet don't make an assumption that those with a Spanish background, who live in the United States, subscribe to the Latin American view of time; for those in business in the United States, regardless of their Spanish heritage, a twelve o'clock appointment for a phone interview means just that: on the dot of twelve.

What about how long each culture expects you to take to draw up a contract, make a deal, or get the documents signed, and the money paid? As noted before, in India the expectations can be that it will take much longer. In some countries that have not yet embraced technology to the extent that the United States, Western Europe, Japan, Australia, and Canada have, where things are still done by hand, it can take a lot longer. But there is still the people element; just because a company has the most up-to-date computer does not mean that the worker whose job it is to print out that document and overnight it, or even whose job it is to send that electronic file, is going to be efficient about doing it.

OTHER WORK RELATIONSHIP CULTURAL CONSIDERATIONS

Other issues to keep in mind: are work relationships kept at a distance in other cultures, or is there a tendency to work with friends? This varies by country and culture and there are also individual differences but certainly in other cultures, such as Japan, there may be a requirement that the relationship comes first, then the business.

Is after-work entertaining or business socializing done at the local pub or at a restaurant, or are coworkers or clients asked to the house for a dinner?

I have observed that there seems to be a growing reluctance to mix entertaining and business with the home environment so that dining out at a restaurant is much more popular than the work-related dinner party or holiday festival at the boss' place. Perhaps this is tied to the post-9-11 mentality that, underneath a lot of new situations, has a tinge of paranoia or fear about personal vulnerability when sharing more about themselves. By meeting at a restaurant or a bar, the meeting takes place on neutral territory; neither can be judged by their home or even by their work office circumstances.

VACATION AND HOLIDAY CONCERNS

If you do business internationally, you need to consider vacation and holiday concerns, not just if you are traveling for business but if you are placing a call, waiting on information to finish up a report, or sending an e-mail and waiting for a response.

If possible, have an auto responder that will inform those who send you e-mails that you are observing a holiday and are unavailable. Be as specific as possible about how long the holiday lasts and when you will be back at work. Here's an example of an e-mail auto responder from a company based in Seoul, Korea: "We have a national holiday (the Lunar New Year's Day) from 24th to 27th January. We will be back to work on 28th and will follow up when we get back. Best regards,"

Chapter Eight

● ● ●

Coping With a Difficult
Person or Emotion

It *used to be that if you* could not get along with someone at work, if they were making your life miserable, you might just look for another job. With the tight job market today, or if you are an older worker and you are close to retirement so you need to stay at a particular job so you get the maximum company benefits, that option does not exist for you. In this chapter you will learn strategies to cope with demanding people and gut-wrenching emotions because of work relationships so you have a better chance at staying on the job, leaving on your own terms when or if you choose to depart.

Strategy #45
Handling a Toxic Co-Worker or Boss

Linda used to love her job as head of a community center until she had to supervise someone who was dissatisfied with his job title and salary. He made accusations against Linda, including a charge that she hit him, and a four-year legal battle ensued including an investigation by the EEOC (U.S. Equal Employment Opportunity Commission). Just a few years away from retirement, Linda could not quit because she needed to remain to get her full benefits, nor was there anywhere else in the agency where she could transfer. Says Linda, "During this period, I developed high blood pressure, diabetes, angina, and serious jaw pain, all of which needed medical attention."

After much angst and mental torment, the EEOC finally determined that Linda's employee "had no basis for his complaint," but by that time, the ordeal had taken its toll on Linda's reputation, not to mention her health. What did Linda learn from this experience that might help others to avoid a similar situation? She learned to be much more careful about extending herself to an employee especially if she had any suspicions that he had emotional problems. She learned to be much more conscientious about documenting everything that was said and done in the workplace so if there were any discrepancies in a "he said-she said" accusatory discussion, she would at least have something in writing that she could point to. She also learned that she should have gone to her own supervisor first, voicing her concern that her employee might be making unfounded accusations. That way, her superiors would have heard it first from Linda, and they would not have been as surprised when the employee got the jumpstart by pointing the finger.

WHAT CAUSES SOMEONE TO BECOME DIFFICULT?

You have certainly met a grueling person over your lifetime. They range from the obnoxious kid in school who always causes trouble in class, to the coworker who makes your life miserable by wearing the strongest perfume you have ever smelt even though you have told her five times that you are highly allergic.

Why are these individuals difficult? Sometimes it is a temporary situation. A family member is sick or has just died and they are acting out, trying to make everyone else around them as miserable and upset as they are. Oftentimes these individuals have difficult personalities dating back to their earliest years. When others were patted on the back and given kudos for their achievements, these individuals, unable or unwilling to try to get accolades for excelling, found a way to get some attention, albeit negative. Over time, it became a pattern and they grew to expect (even want) to be singled-out for their annoying ways, whether at work or at home.

Because of emotional issues, there are also people who need to get into arguments with everyone, including those with whom they work, in order to recreate the confrontational negative relationships they had during their formative years with parents, caregivers, or siblings. Without therapy or a life-changing event to turn this personality trait around, you will have to deal with this difficult person at work or in business.

Unless your safety or sanity is threatened—see the sections that follows on bullying at work or workplace violence—here are some ways to deal with this work relationship:

- Try ignoring the difficult person's behavior rather than reacting to every single thing and getting into constant confrontations.
- Use kindness to win him or her over. Compliment their work attempt to build up their self-esteem so they do not need to get negative attention.
- If the behavior is completely uncalled for and obnoxious, you can let him or her know that you will not put up with whatever it is that is out of line. Stand your ground. That is what 31-year-old Jessica did when she was project manager. As Jessica explains: "I had a meeting with a staff member from within my division regarding a project nearing completion. The person tried to be intimidating and was very aggressive in her approach about concerns with the project. When I said I'd like to address these concerns as quickly as possible as I was going away for a long period of time, she said 'The office doesn't stop just because you go on leave you know' in which I looked at her in disbelief, shook my head and said, 'You're

unbelievable.' 'What was that?' 'You're unbelievable,' I repeated."

- If the negative behavior persists, let your coworker (or employee) know that you will be forced to go to the boss or to human resources to report what is going on, which you are reluctant to do. Hopefully that will help him or her to curb this annoying behavior.

- If that does not work, you can go to human resources and ask for help with the situation. Ask someone to intervene on your behalf.

DEALING WITH A TOUGH BOSS

What are the images of the boss in popular culture? Take Meryl Streep in the 2006 movie version of "The Devil Wears Prada," with Anne Hathaway playing her young, terrorized assistant. Or the cliché of the overbearing boss in "9 to 5" movie starring Jane Fonda, Lilly Tomlin and Dolly Parton, from the 1980s, but revived and rewritten as a new musical in 2009. Where do you find a strong but nice boss in literature or pop culture? Those examples are harder to find and to emulate.

It is much harder to cope with the difficult person if it's your boss or your boss' boss since they are writing your paychecks. Here are some suggestions:

- If your boss is treating everyone badly, depersonalize the treatment. It is obviously not you so try not to overreact.

- If you feel you have to go to HR or someone above your boss to complain, start documenting comments and actions so you have something concrete rather than only vague statements like, "My boss is saying extremely nasty and mean things to me" or "My boss is making unrealistic demands on me."

- Do you just have to put up with it? That depends on how extreme his or her behavior is. What about the boss who is, simply, bossy? How much of that is his or her discomfort at being in charge, or his or her internalized notion that a boss has to be bossy in order to get respect and to be seen as an authority figure? What if he or she associated kindness and graciousness with weakness and being taken advantage of?

- Sometimes the only way to deal with a difficult boss is to quit. If you are able to get out of the situations, it just might turn out to be a very positive thing. As Judith Kolva, Ph.D., a Florida-based college professor, says, about her former boss: "My boss tried to micro-manage me, which does not work for me. So, I quit." For Judith, however, this led to a very positive career change. She continues: "But in the long run this worked into a situation which led to my Ph.D. which, in turn, is one of the best things that ever happened to me."

TURNING AROUND NEGATIVE RELATIONSHIPS

It's one thing to handle or deal with toxic or negative bosses, co-workers, or employees. It's quite another to turn those relationships into positive ones, perhaps even friends. Yes, it is easier said than done to not just get the toxic worker on your side but turn the toxic worker, whether the boss, a coworker, or an employee, into someone with whom you have a solid, strong, and positive relationship. Here's the good news: I've facilitated situations where this actually happened, or something close to it. What are those strategies that can work? First of all, as tough as it is to actually do, work on winning over your nemesis with kindness. In one situation, where someone's boss was making her life miserable, I asked this person to find out what her boss liked to do. It turned out, he and his wife were opera buffs. I recommended that this employee buy four opera tickets and that she and her husband take her boss and his wife to the opera.

She followed my advice, and the rest is history, as they say. Till her boss retired many years later, their more positive relationship helped that employee not only to shine on the job but to feel more comfortable whenever she was in the office or out in the field.

If opera isn't something that this toxic worker would jump to, how about inviting him out for lunch, dinner, or brunch, either just the two of you or, if it feels appropriate and comfortable, with your spouses or significant others along? This will be especially bonding if you can express the reasons that the four of you would probably enjoy each other's company, such as having attended the same school, grown up in a similar town, city, state, or country, working in a related field, or enjoying the same kind of sports, cultural, or other activity. The worst that can happen is that he says "no," ignores your request, he says "yes" but then cancels at the last minute, or the get together happens and is a disaster. If you can get this toxic worker to actually break bread with you, whether it is just you or you plus one other, you are most likely in for a very pleasant surprise in how it will benefit your relationship. The toxic worker actually craves attention and having strong bonds but her fear of being abandoned, and deep seated feelings of insecurity, cause her to push people away when she really wants to pull them closer. If you understand this psychological dynamic and do the opposite by trying to connect rather than running away, you may actually break through this toxic worker's grip on you as you become not just colleagues who respect each other but even friends.

Second of all, resist just "taking it" when your toxic worker boss, coworker, or employee dishes out their venom. Most everyone else quakes in their boots when this type throws their weight around. They actually have more respect for those who stand up to them than for those who just take it because they fear the repercussions for writing or speaking their mind. Whether you do it in person, over the phone, or in an e-mail, make sure you let this toxic worker know that you will not be victimized. (But be very careful and reread any e-mails that you plan to send, and choose your words wisely in any verbal exchanges you have or plan to have, since you do not want your justified courage to be used against you either informally at the workplace or, even worse, in a court of law, so to speak.)

Third of all, bestow compliments and attention on this toxic worker to the nth degree which means make sure you remember his birthday, give her as lavish a holiday gift as possible without being too outrageous or violating any ethics rules in terms of how much money you are allowed to spend, tell him he's terrific at least once a day, and you will see this toxic worker starting to bring you that much closer into his inner circle. The compliments have to, of course, come from your heart but if you truly feel that way, but this toxic worker's negativity has just pushed it all down very far in your heart and mind, force yourself to bring it to the surface. This will also help to turn the toxic worker into someone with whom you have a relationship because you are giving the toxic worker what he really needs which is attention, approval, and love.

Fourth, for some toxic workers for whom money is the end all and be all of their existence, and how they measure their success, make lots of money for him or her. However, no matter how much money some toxic workers have, however, they need more. They tend to watch every penny, whether they are just scraping by as a small business owner, a millionaire with several businesses, or head of a major corporation and they are pulling in a six or seven figure salary but they are also responsible for the prosperity of the whole shebang. If you are an insurance salesman, bring in that huge account that will bring hundreds of thousands to your firm and take your vampire boss out for lunch to celebrate. If you work in fundraising for a hospital, get the biggest donors and bring your success to the attention of this toxic worker who is making your life miserable. He will be able to brag about your financial success which will help him look better but also help your relationship with him because you are showing that you value what the toxic worker values – money – which means you also value him. "Getting" what someone needs and wants, and giving it to him or her, is another way of turning that negative or non-existent work relationship into a positive one.

Now of course you could try all four of these suggestions and the toxic worker is still so unbearable that you will just put up with him or her until you find a new job and can quit. But at least even if you cannot win her or him over with these strategies, you will always know that you truly tried to turn the situation around, and even befriend this person rather than just taking it and throwing in the towel on a truly challenging work relationship situation. Also beware that by trying one or more of the above tactics you may find that this toxic person, who usually has deep-seated conflicts over intimacy, feelings of competitiveness and jealousy, as well as an approach-avoidance to success, may let you go or even fire you before you are ready to make your next move. So proceed with caution with the above advice since too aggressively trying to turn the toxic relationship into a positive one can backfire big time.

You may find that the more tempered approach is to learn more about what makes this toxic person tick, why he or she is like that, and just put up with him or her until you make other work arrangements that will keep you getting that steady pay check but in a more positive atmosphere. (As you saw in the example of Brenda, at the beginning of the book when I discussed the vampire, who did just that, finding a way to out fox the vampire that she had to deal with at work over so many years.)

Strategy #46
Coping With Jealousy and Competitiveness

A hint of jealousy and competitiveness at work is not necessarily negative and counterproductive. Deal with it by turning it into a motivator. Don't think of it as a negative feeling. Think of it as a positive feeling to motivate you to get whatever it is that you're jealous of whether it's getting a bonus, more attention, or a promotion.

But if jealousy is such a strong feeling that it gets out of hand, it can become a blinding emotion. That feeling, in some instances, can be the force behind sabotaging coworkers, such as intentionally failing to share a phone message with a colleague that leads to a deal going to someone else or, even worse, escalating to physical violence.

The first step when coping with jealousy and competitiveness is to acknowledge that you feel that way (or that someone else feels that way toward you). What might be going on? Are you bragging excessively about your own achievements? Are you flaunting any awards you have received or even dressing in too flashy a way that is directing too much attention to you?

If you are not provoking jealousy and competitiveness in your coworkers or boss, try to understand where they are coming from and why they might be feeling the way they do. It will not lessen the pain you may be feeling because of their behavior, but at least you will see that it has more to do with their own limitations or upbringing or insecurities than it has to do with you.

Strategy #47
Handling the Workplace Bully

Who hasn't encountered at least one workplace bully? "Bob was a workplace bully and so was Valerie although she never bullied me. But she bullied other people" says Mark, a successful executive. "But," he continues, "Sam was a screamer. He actually had to go to anger management class."

Why don't you want to be, or be around, a workplace bully? Mark continues, "They make it uncomfortable for everyone. They terrorize people. They terrorize the workplace. They lead by fear. Sam would lose his temper and it would scare people. They were afraid to go into his office and talk to him because he would explode. That's not good because people tend to keep unpleasant news away from him. Valerie was never satisfied. She would keep people late at night working. She would always change her mind about something. She used to drive everyone crazy. No one wanted to work with her."

You might think that bullies get booted out of corporations. Alas, says Mark, "Valerie's still there. Bullies tend to get promoted. People in charge like to have them around because it tends to make them look good. They use them as hatchet men. They get them to do their dirty work. They make their bosses look good because people can deflect their rage and these people leaving the bosses to be the nice guy."

What are some strategies to deal with workplace bullies? Here are some suggestions if the bully is a coworker, at your same level:

- You don't have to put up with it. You can deal with them directly. You can stand up to them. You can say, "You have no reason to talk to me like that. I want an apology."
- You can go to human resources.

What if the bully is your boss? It's a stickier situation. Human resources might even report to your boss so sharing your grievance with HR might back-fire big time. If you make your accusation or complaint about the bully after the fact, it will be harder to prove its validity since you may have already been fired and it will be seen more as a "sour grapes" response. Here are some possible ways to deal with the bully boss:

- Stand up to your bully boss. If you don't stand up to your boss even though he or she is a bully, things will get worse. Just as bullies terrorize the schoolyard, they will terrorize the workplace unless you stand up to them. Stand up to them and they can't get to you.
- If the human resource department does not report to your boss, go to them and lodge a complaint.

IF THE BULLY IS A SUBORDINATE

As an article in *HR Magazine* by Kathy Gurchiek points out, bullies may be subordinates who bully their supervisor. A survey, "Managing Conflict at Work," presented at an annual British Psychological Society Symposium on Workplace Bullying, found that 12 percent of the bullying accusations were "made against people the complainants supervise." What form did this bullying take? Some examples of bullying up the ladder were: ignoring a manager's instructions, failing to deliver messages to a manager, making sure papers were not delivered in time to a meeting, and spreading lies about the supervisor,. According to Gary Namie, co-founder of the Workplace Bullying & Trauma Institute, this type of bullying should be dealt with in the following ways:

- If someone is a new manager, avoid saying, "This is how I did it at the last job" because it challenges the status quo.
- Senior management needs to support dealing with the bully because "confronting the bully must be done by a supervisor at least two levels about the targeted boss" since the bullies "respond to power and they respond to organizational pressure."

- The high level manager should let the bully know that his behavior is going to be monitored and if the bullying continues, he or she will be fired.

What if the bully is someone you have to deal with in business? Here are some ways to deal with it:

- Reassess how important this business contact is to you. If you can walk away, consider doing it and finding someone who is not a bully.
- If this business associate has a monopoly on a type of service or product, and you have to deal with this bully, try delegating working with this person to someone who is not bothered by his or her behavior and may have a better relationship with him or her.
- Don't let the bully impact your confidence or your ability to do your job.

Strategy #48
Dealing With Anger at Work

Everyone loses his or her temper, now and then, but this type of anger is best dealt with outside of work. You do not want to get the reputation for being a "hot head." The signs that you are angry at someone at work can be so strong and obvious that it is easy for everyone to know how you're feeling. You may get red in the face, your heart starts racing, and you feel as if you are going to explode. Or the signals may be more subtle, for example, you start coughing and you realize you're not sick but it's really your anger manifesting itself through physical symptoms. "I don't have a good outlet for my anger," says a middle-aged male executive

Here are some strategies for dealing with anger at work at coworkers or a boss so you avoid the increased stress associated with holding in the anger:

- Call and rant to someone, especially someone who is "safe," such as a spouse, friend, or someone outside of the specific workplace environment.
- Take a walk, or work out at the on-site or nearby gym.
- Write about your feelings, but make sure you keep it in a safe place and away from wandering eyes.
- If you feel safe in sharing your feelings with the person who is causing your anger, do so. Be careful not to place blame. Just express how you are feeling and why.

Strategy #49
Becoming More Aware of Workplace Violence

Be aware of the circumstances that you might encounter at work to avoid being one of the estimated 1,000 men and women annually who are victims of workplace violence in the United States (up from 750 persons a year in the 1980s). But it is not just an American problem. In March 1996, a man entered an elementary school in Scotland, randomly shooting and killing one teacher and fifteen children. Canadian businessman Frank Roberts was murdered in 1998 as he arrived at the company he founded in Toronto.

As workplace violence expert Larry Chavez pointed out to me, estimates for work-related violence are even higher if you add in the injuries or deaths because of job-related violence such as taxi cab drivers who are killed on the job or convenience store clerks who are robbed or killed. The lower statistics quoted are for workplace violence in more traditional office settings, such as office buildings.

Although terrorism is of course an act of violence that may occur at work, whether you worked in the World Trade Center back on September 11, 2001, or you work for an embassy that is bombed in another part of the world. But the workplace violence that is more common are the acts of physical violence including rape, assault, homicide, or robbery.

This is not what anyone wants to think about when getting ready for work. Work is where you go and it should be a place where you toil without fear for your personal well being. Here are some examples of workplace violence shared with me through interviews or "ripped" from the headlines:

- An employee at a financial services corporation was being let go but they allowed him to come in and use his office to look for a new job. That employee somehow got a gun into the office and he shot and killed his manager. (This was before the 9-11 terrorist attacks and the heightened security in reaction to those attacks that many companies put in place. Some companies do have metal detectors now.)
- A real estate agent goes to meet a potential buyer at an empty, available property only to find she has been lured there as she finds herself the victim of a rape and robbery.
- A 23-year-old freelance theater reviewer is accosted by a gang on his way home from reviewing an off-off-Broadway play. He is stabbed during the attempted mugging and dies several days later of his wounds.

This section is a key one in this book on work relationships because the Bureau of Labor Statistics, United States Department of Labor, in their 2005 Survey of Workplace Violence prevention found that over 70 percent of United States workplaces did not have a formal program or policy that addressed workplace violence. The study also discovered that almost 86% of the establishments surveyed did not have a security staff. According to this survey, in general, the larger the company, the more likely there is at least one form of security: 99% of businesses with more than 1,000 workers had at least one type of security versus just

64.9% of those businesses with just one to ten workers.

Workplace violence, which includes assault, homicide, robbery, or rape, falls into a couple of categories. The first is where you are simply at the wrong place at the wrong time. Someone comes in off the street and you, or your coworkers, are put in the position of being potential victims of this stranger/perpetrator. In that situation, the key consideration is whether or not the building was secure and if procedures were in place to keep out intruders who might commit violent acts.

Carefully consider the security of where you work, especially if you tend to get in early or leave late. Is it necessary to have a key or security code to get into the building? Are there security guards checking visitors for a photo ID, making sure that no one is allowed into the building who does not have an appointment or a valid reason for the visit? If there is a parking garage, is it well-lit? If you need to leave the building late at night is there anyone available to walk you to your car or, if the building is in an urban area, to a taxi cab or a bus stop, if you are fearful for your safety? Are there working emergency phones that connect to the building security or local police station especially if cell phone service in the area is unreliable if you need to report any suspicious behavior? Does your company offer crime prevention awareness training to help employees to feel more confident that they can assess potentially violent situations before any violence occurs?

That's what your employer and the building where you work could do. What about your own actions? If you are worried about a particular coworker, boss, or any other employee, service provider, client, or customer that you work with, let someone know who might offer some helpful suggestions. Whether it's your boss or human resources, if someone threatens you or hits you, or brandishes a weapon, you need to speak up. Watch out for expressions of homicidal or suicidal ideation; the phenomenon of murder-suicide means that some who are contemplating suicide may first commit homicide to take one or more people along with them at the end.

The goal of this section is not to make you more paranoid but to help you to become more aware so you are less likely to be a victim. Although many find comfort in the idea of the "random" victim which means that no matter what you do a criminal may pick you at random so you can't do anything to make yourself a less likely target or, along the same vein, there are those who find comfort in the "just world hypothesis," the notion that the world is just and as long as you do what is right and just you are unlikely to have tragedy befall you. The just world hypothesis is what helps someone to go to work without the fear that he or she will be shot by a disgruntled coworker or robbed by a desperate former employee.

The truth lies somewhere in-between. Yes, victims, especially if they are strangers, seem to be chosen at random but there are still some red flags that you can watch out for that someone may be out to harm you. In general, most criminals do not want to be caught, despite the notion from Dostoyevsky's classic novel, *Crime and Punishment*, that Raskolnikov was driven by his need to be caught because his conscience could not allow him to get away with murder, literally.

In the "real" world, most criminals do not want to be caught. Career criminals, especially, want their ill-gotten gain and they want to get away with it. Therefore, they are more likely to choose victims they can overpower rather than those who might be able to fight back, leading to their capture, arrest, trial, and incarceration. What that means is that if an office building has excellent security, that building is less likely to be targeted by criminals than buildings where security is lax. If someone is walking through the halls with a pocketbook that is open so that a criminal could just scoop his hand into that pocketbook and take out a wallet, without much effort, that pocketbook is more likely to be targeted than a pocketbook that has a zipper and even a flap that covers over the zipper making it that much harder for a criminal to get the wallet that he plans to rob.

There are no guarantees than anyone can avoid being a victim but you will be a less likely target if you have a heightened awareness whenever you go into an office building or an enclosed structure, whether it is a garage, a school, or a bathroom inside that structure. If you see someone who looks suspicious, certainly avoid getting into a potentially compromising situation where you are alone with this person and there is little chance of escape.

I interviewed Robert Gardner, a California-based independent security consultant who spent 25 years as a policeman. Gardner points out that awareness is one of the keys in preventing workplace violence. As he says:

"One of the things you see, after every employment type violent incident, they go back and interview everybody and people start saying, 'You know what? He was always threatening people.' There are all these red flags that potentially predict what was ultimately going to happen. It's an awareness issue more than anything else. Companies need to have awareness. They need to train their employees to be aware that if they should see something, it should be reported. It must be reported. It's okay to report it. One of the biggest impediments is that people don't want to get involved. 'What if I'm wrong?' They don't report things they should report. There needs to be a process set up, even if it's anonymous. There's also a fear that if they do report it, somehow that's going to adversely impact them. They're going to get sued. They're going to get fired. They're going to be demeaned by upward management as an alarmist. But if it was dealt with, a large majority of the classic kind of workplace violence wouldn't occur."

What are some warning signs that an employee is "at risk?" Gardner sites these situations in "Preventing Workplace Violence: Management Considerations":

- Exhibits emotional instability or violent behavior
- Exhibits signs of extreme stress
- Undergoes profound personality changes
- Feels victimized by supervisors or the organization
- Makes threats or alludes to acts of workplace violence
- Exhibits signs of extreme paranoia or depression
- Displays behavior inappropriate to the situation at hand
- Exhibits signs of drug or alcohol abuse
- Is involved in a troubled, work-related romantic situation

Gardner shared with me that he was working on a case in Las Vegas involving a slot attendant working at a supermarket that was beaten up. It happened at two o'clock in the morning. Other employees, however, had noticed the offender who beat up the employee for at least an hour "acting violently outside, beating up a Coke machine." The offender took apart a supermarket cart and used a piece of the cart to beat up the slot attendant. As Gardner explains: "That supermarket was totally in violation of Nevada law and OSHA. If they had trained their people, this guy would have been dealt with half an hour before he attacked the slot attendant."

What does Gardner suggest if you're face-to-face with a violent situation at work? "Get away from them," he says. "Get out of that situation. If you're trapped one-on-one in the room with them and they're being violent, the best you can do is fight back and hope for the best."

As long as it's legal, Gardner recommends carrying and using pepper spray as a deterrent. He says, "If you spray somebody with pepper spray, they aren't fighting with you anymore. Before pepper spray, they had mace. It didn't work on everyone. But pepper spray is an irritant and it burns the mucous lining the nose and it makes you close your eyes. Once you can't see, you're at a distinct disadvantage."

Gardner emphasizes how effective pepper spray can be when he notes: "If you go hiking in Alaska, that's what you carry with you for the bears. It has a physical reaction that you can't deal with once you've been hit with it."

Some situations to be especially careful about are leaving an office late at night alone and walking into a dark isolated parking garage.

In his experience, cautions Gardner, he has found that "small businesses that suffer a serious workplace violence issue go out of business. One incident and it destroys the company." Although "really really large businesses can weather through that," the key is to avoid being the victim of workplace violence whatever size company you work for.

In summary, here are some suggestions to protect yourself from being the victim of workplace violence:

- Be aware.
- Report anything that seems suspicious.
- Pay attention at all times especially when you are walking to or from work late at night.
- Wear shoes that will enable you to run if you have to.
- Park in well-lit areas that have security surveillance preferably by a guard.
- Ask human resources to have a policy in place about how to deal with suspicions or incidents that make you fearful of workplace violence.
- In an outside office, have a system for monitoring how visitors enter the premises rather than having an open door policy.
- If you have to work late or get in earlier than anyone else, see if someone else will accompany you to and from the office or if an employee or co-worker will also work those hours with you.
- Trust your instincts.

- If you work alone or at home, do not see clients or customers without others around. If necessary, meet clients or customers in a public setting, such as a coffee shop or a restaurant, or rent office space by the hour in an office building with security surveillance and preferably security guards.
- If it's legal, consider carrying pepper spray.

Larry Chavez, who was a police officer for 31 years including being a hostage negotiator, suggests these additional preventive measures: "Because there are so many domestic violence-related workplace incidents whereby a husband, who is separated from his wife and being denied custody of his children, goes to the workplace, where he knows he can find his ex-wife, and he shoots and kills his former partner, and possibly other workers and then himself, do not allow husbands access to their spouses at work. That is what one international company with many offices in California has done. They will not allow a spouse into the building under any circumstances. If he delivers flowers to the front desk and asks to bring the flowers up for his wife's birthday, his permission is denied." Chavez also suggests that any wife or romantic partner who has a restraining order make sure that her supervisor and everyone else at the company knows about that restraining order.

When you first start working at a company, you should locate the exits you could use in the event of a fire, or if someone appeared on the premises threatening violence. If there is no second exit, such as in a high rise building, Chavez recommends creating a safe room that would have a bullet-proof door for protection.

Chavez studied 400 cases of what he calls "internal" workplace violence—that is, violence occurring inside of the office buildings—with which he had been involved since 1966, and these were his results:

- 43.6% involved current employees
- 22.5% involved former employees (who returned to the workplace)
- 21% were domestic disputes that were played out at the workplace
- 12.5% were client relationships

Another interesting statistic from Chavez's study: 95% of all workplace violence incidents were perpetrated by men.

Strategy #50
Affirmations to Help You Deal With Negative Connections

What if you find yourself in a negative work environment, but for whatever reason, you can't quit right now? Previously I mentioned Linda, who had to stick it out in a toxic workplace for a few years until she could retire at full benefits. Others perform such unique jobs that they are unlikely to readily find another similar opportunity especially in a tough economy. There are some who feel they must stay at a particular job even though their coworkers, boss, or clients are causing a lot of daily or regular stress because they are older and the job prospects are tougher past a certain age. There are countless others who feel that working with difficult coworkers or a demanding boss is better than no job at all. There are also entrepreneurs, consultants, or business owners who have clients or customers who are frustrating and challenging to deal with. However, maintaining those client/customer relationships is imperative for professional or economic reasons, at least for the time being.

What follows are some affirmations that you could read or reread to yourself that may help you to survive dealing with those negative work relationships. You could read these affirmations right after a particularly tough incident occurs — perhaps you just received an especially harsh or cruel e-mail from a particular individual — or you could just review one or all of these affirmations from time to time to help you to cope.

Here, therefore, are ten affirmations to help you but of course feel free to add your own as well:

1. I am a terrific, valuable, hardworking employee and I have a right to work in a positive environment.
2. I did not create this difficult situation but I have the strength and forbearance to handle it.
3. I will not allow my boss to drive me out of this job until I am ready to leave on my own terms and within my own time frame.
4. I can handle my coworkers or my boss and there is also the possibility that my boss or coworkers will be replaced with others who are easier to deal with.
5. I do not deserve to work in negative conditions or to be around unpleasant people but I deserve to have this job.
6. I am in control of my reaction to any annoying person or grueling work situation.
7. I am developing my stamina by surviving and even triumphing despite these tough work conditions.
8. I depend on this job and I will not be railroaded out.
9. Others depend on me to have this job and I will do it to the best of my ability.
10. I feel sorry for the difficult person or persons who are making my life miserable but I will not allow their problems to become my own troubles or to ruin my job performance.

Strategy #51
Benefit From Harsh Feedback About Your Work

Receiving criticism is never easy. If someone criticizes you or gives you excessively harsh feedback that you have to deal with or you will lose your job, try some of these "recovery techniques":

- Take a deep breath and resolve to deal privately with your angst, rage, and disappointment. Don't let this person see how upset she or he has made you.
- Figure out what personality type you are dealing with (see Chapter 2). That will help you to understand why this person is mishandling his or her supervisory role so you won't take those actions personally.
- Put your ego aside and separate out what is vicious and malicious and what is valuable about the comments or criticism you have received that might actually be useful.
- Take a deep breath and deal with this person over the phone, in person, or through e-mail. How can you make your work relationship more personal and positive so that the outcome will be more constructive?
- If you have to work with this person on a project or in the same department, write down your goal for your relationship. Keep your eye on that goal. Keep the personality issues and hurt feelings out of it so you can achieve that goal. Remind yourself of that goal whether it's to keep this job because you and your family need the money, or to excel at this project so you get kudos and maybe even a raise.
- If your anger is so severe that you are afraid of what might happen if you talk with this person face-to-face, but you know that is the best way to try to improve the situation, ask an advocate (or another employee) to join you when you meet with this person, or to be on the line when you speak so you are on a conference call.
- Under all circumstances, avoid writing and sending an angry e-mail or calling and saying anything you will regret saying the next day. If you have to "vent," do it in a journal or write something and file it, destroy it, or, if you

need to share it with a trusted family member of friend, do so but *do not send it*. And avoid sharing with anyone at work who might use it against you.

- Remember: do not respond to the venom or the character assassinations. Do not allow this person to destroy your confidence, this project, or your career. Diffuse the situation by responding, simply, with words like this: "Thank you for your detailed feedback. I will carefully consider all of your suggestions and respond to each point that you raised as soon as possible."

- Keep your initial response short and sweet. You can deal with all the myriad of detailed comments soon enough. Right now, everyone is watching to see if you can take criticism or if you will blow up, throw in the towel, and remove yourself from this project or even from dealing with this person at all. Do not let that happen! Once again, if you do that, he or she wins and you lose. It may feel good temporarily not to deal with this person, but it will hurt you and your career. Especially if you don't have another job lined up, you will be out of work and miserable. If you leave, leave on your own terms and in your own time. You stay in control even though this person is definitely trying to control you.

- Is this guaranteed to turn the situation around in your favor? Unfortunately, there are no guarantees. But you can at least try to work with this person to get the positive outcome that is in everyone's best interest, especially yours. This person does not have to become your new best friend. He or she cannot be allowed to sabotage your project, your reputation, or your career. Put all your energy into turning the situation around. You can do it! I'm one of many who are on your side even if it seems this person and even others are not.

Print out this list and keep it within easy reach!

Strategy #52
Using Meditation to Reduce Stress

Another strategy to deal with negative work relationships is to meditate. David Wagner, a Manhattan-based educator who teaches meditation through his company, Banyan Education, offers this advice for how you can use meditation to deal with a difficult workplace situation if you are unable to quit:

"When people have a strong connection to their being, to their core self, then they are able to have a kind of leverage in those situations so they can decide: 'How much do I want this to affect me?' In other words, people start to participate in it. What I see with my clients is that they start to know themselves in a way that there is a part of them that is independent of what's going well and what's going terribly in their life. If someone treats us badly, we feel bad. If we're unhappy in work or a relationship, it automatically goes all the way through us. Maybe it is a negative work environment and it's unchangeable. But we can always have this idea in our mind, intellectually, that this doesn't affect me, I shouldn't take it personally."

Strategy #53
Adios (Good-bye if Leaving is the Best Option)

Even if you cannot quit this instant, you can at least start looking for a new job. If you want to hold out till you retire, you can put your non-work time into planning for your retirement, proactively considering what you will do once you are free of this negative environment.

Jill had an overly demanding and toxic boss who turned on her. She put up with it for three years but she saw the handwriting on the wall and she knew it was best to leave rather than get fired. She left on her own terms. Two other account managers did not heed the warning signs and they were fired. Because Jill left when she wanted to, she was able to set herself up with freelance assignments since there was never any question about her previous work situation. Her two former coworkers, however, had to admit that they were let go which usually closed the next door on their face. Three years later, Jill shares that they are both struggling. Neither has found a new job yet. One of the fired account managers, an Ivy League graduate, has been living off of savings and the generosity of friends and family members. The other has occasional short-term assignments but she's gained thirty pounds and is still upset about her work situation. Leaving before the axe fell is definitely a strategy that Jill is glad she utilized. Here is more of Jill's story in her own words:

> Of course, please don't use my name. I'd hate for him to see this. Initially, he thought I walked on water. But he truly had a pathological personality disorder. He was extremely insecure and if you made a mistake, he'd go ballistic because he felt it reflected badly on him. Everyone was just miserable and he used these intimidation techniques on everyone. So when I made a mistake, since I am not perfect, he turned on me, and suddenly nothing I did was right.
>
> Initially, I tried to work my way out of it, working overtime, etc. I'd always excelled so it was quite a comedown to have everything I did subjected to relentless scrutiny and criticism. And the problem is that you start second-guessing yourself so much that you lose your bearings. And in the end, I don't think I was doing such great work because he had so undermined my confidence. I finally realized there was no way out.
>
> Thank goodness I'm entrepreneurial and knew I'd be fine once I got out of there. I gave notice during the evaluation—which he offered to change when I quit!!!

Which is extremely telling. But I had already made up my mind. I had been unhappy for a long time and I could see that he was just toxic. But I stayed on for 3 months more until they found my replacement and when I left, he asked me to continue doing the twice monthly syndicated medical column I had been writing while on staff—which I continued to do for another two years. Until—drum roll please—he finally got fired...[a]fter the remaining staffers got together and went en masse to his boss demanding that they can him. And he's since been fired from the job he got after that—his wife dumped him, etc. Truly bad news. But my only alternative was to quit—and a good thing I did. Not to break my arm patting myself on the back. He gave me not a great evaluation (which I know was his way of motivating his staff to do better). But I had been very unhappy at the job and he was just a tyrant. Morale was incredibly low in the section. I kept hoping they'd fire him but they didn't while I was there. I hadn't been there long enough to have any credibility with the higher ups, so I was just stuck. Like I said, a good thing I left of my own accord. Two other very talented account managers did not....But I saw the handwriting on the wall. And as a result, I left on good terms, didn't burn any bridges, continued to write a syndicated column and did occasional freelance pieces for the health section for many years afterwards. Hopefully, this is helpful.

Sometimes bosses are just too toxic and you've got to know when to hold 'em, and know when to fold 'em. And I folded—but not before I had made a couple of trips to New York hustling work, etc. So the transition from the job to freelancing was almost seamless. Like I said, I don't want to break my arm patting myself on the back. But looking back, I think I made the best of an intolerable situation.

Therefore, even if you would like to stay at your current job because it is a good work opportunity, but you have tried really hard to deal with the work relationships and you know in your heart of hearts that you just need to move on, leaving this company may be the best strategy for you. (See Chapter 10, Building a Better Career, for suggestions on how to use social media sites to reconnect with previous coworkers or bosses and to find a new job.)

Chapter Nine

Working Alone But Not Lonely

Strategy #54
Participate in a Mastermind or Other Peer Group

Seven years ago Stefan Doering was crossing a street in Brooklyn with the light when a car making a left turn almost hit him. He remembers going up to the driver's side and leaning over to say something when, according to witnesses, the driver threw open the car door, then got out of the car and punched Stefan, which caused him to fall back and fracture his skull on the cement pavement.

Stefan has "zero memory of this" but witnesses later told him that the driver got back into his car and took off. Soon afterwards, Stefan was raced to the hospital where doctors didn't know if the 37-year-old entrepreneur was going to live or die. He was in the intensive care unit (ICU) for six days and in a coma for at least five. A week later, Stefan was released from the hospital.

His first memory after the accident was three weeks later, at his parent's house on Long Island. There was a party going on, celebrating that he was alive. Says Stefan: "I had lost my vision, my hearing, and I could not walk. Doctors didn't think I would ever be able to walk again."

But Stefan, determined to prove the doctors wrong, turned to his Mastermind group, which is a group of peers who meet by phone or in person on a regular basis to help each other to achieve their goals. This particular group was made up of seven men and women who met when they had each completed a six-month intensive training program on self-growth. After that, they banded together to meet weekly to take their development to the next level. They called themselves The Soaring Geese.

"We named our group after how geese fly in a flock in a *v* formation," explains Stefan. "They do that because the head goose breaks the wind turbulence so it takes a lot less energy when they're flying in the same direction. When you hear geese flying overhead, they're honking. That honking is their form of communication, saying to the goose in the front, 'I'm here.'"

"I wanted to create an unreasonable goal for myself," says Stefan, "so I told my group that I didn't just want to walk again, I wanted to run five miles in Central Park in ninety days."

One of Stefan's closest friends, Rick Mavrovich, who was also in the Mastermind group, says, "Our immediate reaction was we were just stunned. We thought this guy is crazy! He's a naïve optimist. Someone did recommend he should have smaller goals and work his way up to it. But Stefan said 'no.' That was his goal and he wanted us to support him. Once he convinced us it was his goal, we aligned ourselves with him."

Another member of the Mastermind group, Manhattan-based public relations executive Catherine Saxton, remembers visiting Stefan in the hospital and also being there for him during his recovery time as he basically had to learn how to do everything all over again. Says Catherine: "Stefan knew that we were all dedicated to his recovery and to the common goal of supporting and helping each other through the good times and the bad."

Stefan began to train. He explains: "I got frustrated a lot but every time I was ready to give up on my dream of running again, the group was there for me. There was one point before the accident I was running a seven-minute mile. I used to run five miles in about thirty-five minutes. But after the accident, I couldn't run even one mile. I went to the group and said, 'There's no way I can do this.' One of the members said, 'Why are you running?' My knee-jerk reaction was to say, 'I want to prove my doctors wrong.' But they kept asking, 'Stefan, why are you *really* running? What's your purpose? What's your commitment?' The answer was: I was running because I *could* run. I was running because I was alive. That shifted my purpose. As soon as I let go of thinking that I had to get my time better, I started to run."

Eighty-seven days after he announced his "unreasonable" goal to his group, Stefan was in Central Park, along with twenty-two of his friends, family, and members of The Soaring Geese. "I don't know how fast I was running but it didn't matter to me anymore," said Stefan, who now runs BestCoaches Inc., a company that helps set up Mastermind groups. "I ran my five miles to my doctors' amazement. It was six months after the accident and three months after declaring my unreasonable goal."

"I met up with them at the victory meal at a Mexican restaurant," says Sue Gilad, another member of The Soaring Geese who is now a financial coach. "I hadn't doubted that Stefan would succeed at completing the race. He declared it so and the group was holding him accountable to it."

Stefan's story is, of course, inspiring, but it also emphasizes the extraordinary combined added incentive when a goal is shared. We all need others to help us to become the best we can be at work and in business. Whether you work in an office with dozens or hundreds of others, or you toil over a computer in your home office, all alone, we are all still interdependent on other people to succeed—be they coworkers, supervisors, the boss, employees, clients or customers, and even vendors or service providers.

Other Mastermind groups help solo workers to feel less lonely. Louellen S. Coker, President of Content Solutions in Texas, says: "As a small business owner, participation in a Mastermind group is one of the most beneficial aspects of my WBODC (Women Business Owners of Denton County) membership. Over the four years our group has met, I've developed very deep and lasting relationships with women and business owners with whom I probably would not have otherwise. As I've grown from being the only person in my business to managing five employees and various contractors (much of that in the last two months), these women have helped me to define the direction in which I want the company to grow."

There are as many types of Mastermind groups as there are associations, but most adhere to a few basic principles. A key consideration for all Mastermind groups is that everything shared (whether via telephone or in-person) is confidential. Frequency is another concern: will the group meet weekly, bi-weekly or monthly? (Bi-weekly or monthly seem to be the preferred frequency.) National associations, by necessity, with members spread out throughout the country, tend to be phone or virtual groups; regional or local chapters meet in-person if that is the consensus, or by phone, or a combination of the two.

Most groups seem to agree that it is not as important how many people want to be in the group, but that after those initial members start to bond, whether it's three, six, ten, or fifteen, that new members are not added. (If an additional member is to be added, everyone in the current group has to agree on the change.)

Another basic issue is whether or not the group will have a facilitator—leader—or not. The Mastermind group that I participated in for about a year definitely benefited from the leadership of Julia Marrocco, who facilitated our group by setting up the logistics of the bi-weekly calls with the conference call company, sending out meeting reminders, and helping to keep us on track so we shared the allotted time and stayed on schedule so we did not go over our agreed-upon hour.

There are a few aspects to being in a Mastermind group to consider. It can be time-consuming; it's a commitment of energy and focus. If there is one person who is overly competitive, who hogs the time that has to be shared, or there is in-fighting between members, this can lead to frustration and discontent. It can also cause one or more members to badmouth the offender or for the entire group to get a negative impression of someone, his or her business that could be hard to dispel, or the Mastermind group process in general.

Another consideration: if the skills levels among members are disparate, then those who are successful may feel they are not being challenged by those who are neophytes. Mastermind group members may also unwittingly send someone in the wrong direction in his or her career or business.

But the potential positives are very compelling. As Stephanie Chandler, an author and speaker in Gold River, California, notes: "Since forming my Mastermind group, I have increased my rates and have far more clarity about the direction of my business." Rosemarie Rossetti, Ph.D., President of Universal Design Living Laboratory, notes about her Mastermind group through the National Speakers Association: "It was because of my first Mastermind group that my husband and I are building a national demonstration home in Columbus!"

It is crucial not to get discouraged if you join a Mastermind group and it doesn't work out, or if you outgrow a group and have to move on. Shel Horowitz, an author and publisher, notes: "The first Mastermind group I was in was organized by our local National Writers Union chapter. We met over lunch in local restaurants and just talked about our progress and our goals. People stopped showing up or people became very hard to schedule and it just petered out. But I remain friends with several of the people in that group."

JOINING ASSOCIATIONS OR PAID NETWORKING CLUBS

An alternative to more structured and demanding Mastermind group membership is being part of an association of like-minded professionals or workers and participating in the meetings of the local chapter. These activities are another way to substitute for the loss of day-to-day connections if you do not work in a traditional office environment. It can also help to keep you in the loop about what is new in your industry or field as members from across the country or from around the world share about trends at annual conferences, or locally or regionally at local chapter meetings.

Getting involved is going to help you to make the most of any association membership. Just showing up once a year for the conference, or even once a month for the chapter meeting, will make it hard to form any kind of meaningful bonds that could serve as a substitute for that coworker or shared work experience. If you volunteer to be on a committee, you will at least have the opportunity to access other members in-between meetings by phone or e-mail.

Volunteer to be on a committee if no one proactively invites you to join their cause. Practically every committee can use another member unless there are strict guidelines about how many members can serve on a committee, and for what duration. You can pick a committee that reflects what your talents and interests are, such as publicity or fundraising, or you can pick an area where you would like to grow your skills, such as social networking activities or running the internship program.

PAID NETWORKING CLUBS

BNI, Business Networking International, is a way for entrepreneurs who work alone, or small business owners to get together weekly. There is an annual membership fee and each local chapter has the rule that members cannot be from a competing industry; there can only be one real estate agent, printer, videographer, and so forth. Each week one member presents about his or her business so the other members get to know what that individual offers. It is a group that is as much for growing business through referrals as it is for forming relationships but it has the benefit of meeting weekly compared to many national associations with local chapters that usually only meet monthly. The BNI relationships may grow into friendships, even if casual ones, because of the requirement that members attend weekly (or find a replacement for their slot for that week).

Another paid networking group that CEOs may find helpful is Vistage, also known as TEC (The Executive Committee), which has more than 14,500 members in 16 different countries. Vistage enables CEOs to get together with their peers in a facilitated group to share about their similar challenges and best practices.

"To encourage the members to be as open as possible regarding any business matter there are no competitors, suppliers, or clients in the group," says Linda Swindling, JD, formerly a Dallas Vistage chairperson who now speaks on negotiating like a CEO. (An interesting note is that chairs are also in their own Vistage groups.)

In our interview, Linda shared some examples of how Vistage had helped CEO and other key executive members in the three groups she facilitated. She told me about a CEO who had health challenges. The group confronted him and he did something about the problem. Linda says: "He told me it may have saved his life. He got the surgery that he was putting off." She continues: "Another Chief Executive was very successful but he had another business idea that he had kept in a drawer for over a decade. After hearing one of the Vistage speakers talk, he pulled that plan out, began the new business and it cash flowed the first year."

DEALING WITH THE POTENTIAL LONELINESS OF THE LONG-DISTANCE WORKER

How can you work alone without being lonely or disconnected to the workplace or others in your business or industry? There has been a definite growth in the number of workers who are working at home or on their own, whether some or all of the work week, as well as an expanding need to communicate with, and deal with, distant employees or outsourced workers nationally and even internationally. It's not just outsourcing office functions to India or other countries that has to be considered. There are also employees who, because of quality of life or personality issues, prefer to work from home, checking in with the parent office virtually or in-person on an occasional basis, as well as companies that need distant workers to survive economically because of cost or other logistical reasons. The increase of those working independently from home, whether or not they are affiliated with a main office, also continues to rise. Working from home may help with childcare or cutting down on the time or cost of commuting, but it also opens up the challenge of how workers in this situation may maintain relationships with fellow workers as well as supervisors or bosses still at the main office or also working from home or in other locations. Those who are completely independent need help developing and maintaining peer relationships through associations or networking events so they are not completely isolated and alone.

Peter Linkow, Research Leader of New York-based Conference Board's Research Working Group on Managing a Distant Workforce and President of WFD Consulting, surveyed managers and employees in five companies on key issues including managing relationships and connections that need to be addressed with the growth of the distant workforce. In his report, "Managing Across Language, Culture, Time, and Location," Linkow shares his findings that anyone who works away from a traditional nine-to-five office, whether on an occasional or permanent basis, may find useful. Freelancers and those who are self-employed have been dealing with the challenge of being a distant workforce" as one of the realities of their job situation. What is relatively new, with the widespread use of the Internet turning even the most local company into an international one, as well as the accessibility to the parent company that having a cell phone and fax machine opens up, major corporations are dealing with the benefits and challenging of having a distant workforce.

Among the companies studied—Eli Lilly, DuPont de Nemours International, Target Sourcing Services/AMC, Sybase, and Bechtel—over 80% of the employees and managers surveyed work from distances that are more than three hours away from the main office, and almost half work six or more hours' distance.

One of the most intriguing findings of this useful study is the agreement among those surveyed that "the telephone, even more than face-to-face, is the most effective method for developing and maintaining working relationships."

Question: When is the last time you made the conscious decision that you would pick up the phone to call someone instead of sending an e-mail?

Linkow found that employees and managers who worked most effectively in an off-site team shared these five traits:

1. Meet in person at least once a year.
2. Have clear agreements on accessibility.
3. Make good use of group software.
4. Receive sufficient support from the company.
5. Team members have plainly defined roles.

Marilyn Zielinski, Vice President of International Infrastucture and Technology Operations in MetLife's Enterprise Technology Solutions organization, is featured in one of the case studies that Linkow shares in his report on managing distant employees. Zielinski runs two data centers in the United States as well as hosting facilities in Singapore and Mexico City. Zielinski's office is in Hartford, Connecticut, but she is at Met Life Headquarters in New York every Tuesday for a meeting and at Renasselaer or Scranton on Thursday. She goes to each international facility every four months.

Zielinski has five ways that she is able to effectively supervise her distant staff:

1. Having a prescribed staff meeting structure.
2. Putting the right people in the right places.
3. Crossing language and cultural barriers.
4. Being accessible.
5. Possessing a finely crafted management style.

In Linkow's report, Zielinski shares in detail on each of these five strategies for managing two organizations in two different places in the United States as well as with facilities and employees in other countries, Singapore and Mexico City. In terms of structured staff meetings that occur at a distance, meetings should never be scheduled when someone would be sleeping; that time should be sacred. Agendas should be made available in advance to all participants. Responsibilities need to be "clearly articulated" and it is pivotal not to be "U.S.-centric" but to understand and respect other cultures. To do that, Zielinski "relies on people in-country to articulate the dos and don'ts and to identify hot button issues."

Being accessible 7 a.m. to 7 p.m. on weekdays is expected although weekends are off limits except for Sunday night when "Asia is working on our Sunday." Her management style is to be responsive, accessible, and to meet her direct reports face-to-face when she is traveling to the distant sites.

Strategy #55
Coping With the "Lonely at the Top" Boss Syndrome

Public relations executive Harold Burson shared with me in our interview about the lonely at the top perspective when he said, "I think it's a lot easier to be very socially active at lower levels of the company than at the upper levels. One of the prices that you pay for being a CEO in a company is you give up a lot of the social relationships within the company. There's a line beyond which you cannot go."

Is the "lonely at the top" thesis valid? Thirty-seven-year-old Anthony Migyanka, an Irving, Texas-based Managing Partner of Mobile Money Minute, notes: "As the CEO of two prior startups I founded, I agree that sometimes 'Heavy lies the crown,' and 'it's lonely at the top.' My advice to CEOs is: 1. You asked for this, now you got it. Accept your role in that cause/effect relationship. 2. Make a friend. Find a consigliore, a 'number two,' a friend, or a therapist. Someone you can spill to. You can't keep it all to yourself. 3. Realize that no matter how many friends you have, even a good second, you are the driving force for your company, and your company is or will be a reflection of your values, attitudes, and personality."

Vancouver, Canada-based Mark Hamilton used to run a company with sixty people. Now he runs a startup company, "Just Ask Baby," with his wife. Says Hamilton: "The first painful lesson I learned about the isolation of being CEO was to understand *why* it is so lonely. Once you understand the real reason, it is easier to cope. You can never really be friends with the people who work for you. You have too much influence over their career, and you always know that a day may come where you will have to make a decision that may be right for the company, but damaging to them as individuals. That said, this was not where the real isolation comes from. It was from being the only person in the company who was really responsible for the overall business's survival. That responsibility is the same whether you have five employees or five thousand.

"I learned to accept that as CEO your job is not to be liked, it is to be respected, and that if you attempt to be liked, you are failing your primary responsibility which is to the company's success. When you attempt to be liked, you will compromise what is right for the company to make individuals happy.

"For me to live with the isolation, I needed to first accept that the isolation was inevitable and probably required, and then to manage it in a way that was congruent with my values. Being a CEO is a lonely thankless job, and if you cannot live with that, don't take the job."

Although other CEOs join associations or go to meetings with other CEOs, that solution did not work for Hamilton. Instead he found his own way of coping with the isolation "by avoiding meetings with other CEOs in our industry, where possible, and when, I had to go, to stay very quiet and to only listen." Those years he was CEO to a company of sixty, turning to his wife when he needed to share about work matters offered Hamilton the support and reprieve from "the lonely at the top" syndrome that can plague most CEOs.

Chapter Ten

◉ ◉ ◉

Building a Better Career

$\mathscr{S}$*trategy #56*
Use Social Networking to Improve Your Work Relationships

Social networking sites are no longer just for teenagers; savvy workers at all levels are using these sites to develop and strengthen their business relationships as well as to reconnect with previous coworkers or bosses or reach out to new business connections. Just how big is this phenomenon? In February 2009, the most popular site for business networking, LinkedIn.com, which started in 2003, had 35 million users globally; Facebook.com, which started in 2004, had approximately 175 million users and myspace.com, which started in 2003 but is less popular for business networking, had 236 million users worldwide. In 2006, twitter.com joined the online networking world; another business relationship favorite, by 2009 had more than 55 million visitors.

LINKEDIN.COM

LinkedIn.com is a free social networking website that was set up by individuals who seem to understand the benefits of what is known as a "warm" lead. A warm lead is when you approach someone to whom you have some sort of a connection. This is very distinct from what is known as the "cold call" whereby you pick up the phone and contact anyone and everybody without having a specific referral.

Sales experts used to offer a lot of advice on how to master the cold call. More recent sales mavens, however, recommend pursuing warm leads. LinkedIn.com is perfect for those warm leads because you create a profile and then you create a connection to someone by asking them to become part of your network. If they accept your invitation, they become a 1st connection. You and that individual are linked directly. But you can also ask that 1st connection to provide an introduction to their connections so that those connections that are only a secondary (2nd) connection could become a new primary one.

Those are the dual strengths of LinkedIn.com: connecting or reconnecting to someone you already know and then asking that person to help you to expand your network through connecting to their network. You can also read through the profiles of those on LinkedIn.com and approach someone with whom you would like to connect but it is much harder that way, and not even recommended, since the referral system helps to "break the ice" and to try to increase the likelihood that you will be associating with only trustworthy people.

Jake Wengroff got his current job through a family friend with whom he had reconnected through LinkedIn. His friend told him that they were looking for someone at her company. Through his friend, Jake applied for the opening and eventually he was hired.

How do you stand out on LinkedIn? You want your profile to be complete, for starters. That means that you have a photo, a thorough listing of your educational background, current and previous places of employment, as well as what you are looking for through LinkedIn such as getting back in touch, job leads, requests for expertise, and other categories. Recommendations are a way to get noticed. If you want to apply for a job through the free LinkedIn job postings, you may find that having at least one or more recommendations is a requirement for applying for certain jobs.

Jan Wallen, a Connecticut-based speaker and LinkedIn expert, whose been on the site since 2005 and who is the author of *Mastering LinkedIn in Seven Days*, points out that you want your summary section to be enticing and appealing. It should not read like a resume. Says Wallen: "This is where people look to get to know who you are, not simply your credentials. People are going to hire someone that they know, like, and trust. That's where you're building the trust. If they see what they like, they'll look down at your credentials. If your summary doesn't catch their attention, they'll skip your credentials. If you were networking in person, the summary is like the handshake and introduction to someone."

Another way to use LinkedIn more effectively, Wallen notes, is to edit the Public Profile that you will initially be assigned, which includes a series of numbers, to include your name at the end. Then, include that profile whenever you send an e-mail to someone, to help send more people to your LinkedIn profile leading to more potential connections.

Jake Wengroff shared with me this tip about how you can use LinkedIn.com to help yourself to stand out as you grow your reputation as an expert. At the top of LinkedIn.com, on the home page, you will find a couple of boldface headings: People, Jobs, Answers, and Companies. What Jake suggests is that you go to the heading *Answers* and you look at what people are asking. By taking the time to answer questions that have been posted in any of a number of categories—Jake only answers in areas where he has expertise—he is developing a global reputation as an expert in those areas. Here are some of the areas where questions can be asked, and answered, at LinkedIn.com: administration, business travel, financial markets, international, product management, professional development, and Using LinkedIn.

LinkedIn is free but you want to make sure you use your time on it wisely. Canadian-based networking coach Michael Hughes is mainly using LinkedIn to grow his international network as he sets his sights on a more global business. He explains: "LinkedIn has allowed me to connect with people in

Australia, South Africa, and in the United Kingdom and actually start or nurture a bit of a relationship that I would not have done without it."

Ben Thompson, who has a company, Studiofluid, that specializes in branding and website design has found that LinkedIn "has been an extremely valuable tool for me to reconnect with acquaintances and contacts from previous jobs, and has led to a substantial amount of income for my company last year. It has been a natural way to reintroduce myself and create a starting point for new business relationships."

Rick Brenner, who has more than 350 connections on LinkedIn, and who heads a company called Chaco Consulting, uses LinkedIn to grow his business relationships as he cautions: "Never forget that it's about relationship. You can have a million LinkedIn contacts but if there are no relationships behind them they aren't worth that much."

Additional LinkedIn tips to consider:

- Once you are connected to someone, go to their connections and see what you might want an introduction to. Of course be careful about which ones you ask about and also how many you request at once. Maybe one or two at a time, spread out over a couple of weeks or months, rather than asking your new connection with 300 connections of their own to introduce you to their whole network all at once.

- Be careful about who you approach for connections. Especially if you are an independent contractor with multiple projects being juggled all at once, remember that everyone in your network will receive daily updates of anything that you change to your profile especially your answer to the question, "What are you working on?" Make sure whatever you write in that little box you want every single person in your network to be aware of.

- Update your profile every once in a while and everyone will see that updated profile.
- Have as complete a profile as possible including a photo, recommendations, and information on your education, employment, as well as what you are looking for.
- Show an interest in others. Don't just focus on yourself.
- Be careful that you do not seem too aggressive or completely business or sales oriented.
- Remember it's all about people and relationships so use LinkedIn to reconnect, develop, cultivate, or initiate relationships.

Another social networking site that is primarily for business contacts is **xing.com**, which tends to have more European and international than U.S. participants. The basic service is free but you can also pay for a premium version, similar to the graduated free-to-paid-premium-services step up scales for Linkedin.com.

FACEBOOK.COM

There are some, including me, who prefer to use Facebook.com for mainly connecting to personal friends and family. But there are others who use it for business networking as well. Dr. Wendy Guess finds Facebook has helped her to expand her business relationships. She explains: "Oddly enough I was looking for traffic and to build more connection outside of my little circle of friends. I had e-mail lists of friends. I got on there and of course went through the regular round of the people I know. I had a computer geek friend who decided I needed to get on some of the games applications that Facebook has and so I did and found that in the game—I picked the game Pirates—you're building your crew so to speak so you add people as friends in the crew. So I quickly found that I was getting people from all around the world and I'll take it a step further, take it to my high school connection, my college connection. Spurred to connect with more and more people. The people from my past have actually provided resources that I was looking for in my business."

Tim Frick is a 43-year-old Chicago-based entrepreneur who runs a website design company called Mightybytes. Frick shared with me in our interview that he had been running his company for about ten years when he starting doing the social media sites. Says Frick, "After a few months, I noticed a significant difference in the traffic to our site and the number of people I was interacting with on a daily basis changed, the latter due primarily to joining groups on various social sites and answering/posing questions within those groups."

Frick continues: "Facebook is a perfect example of the gray area between business and personal. My Facebook 'friends' are split about 50/50 between business contacts and personal friends. I've always tried to maintain some level of personal information on my profile that is not just promotional information. For example, my company brewed beer this year, we performed in bands, we gave seminars, some of us acted in plays, spoke at conferences, modeled in hair shows, and so on. While some of these things were directly business-related, some weren't. I don't typically differentiate between business and personal on Facebook, primarily because I think including this information shows that we are well-rounded individuals who enjoy a variety of things and would be fun to talk to, not just single-minded workaholics who only want to promote our business."

Frick's business relationships, as well as his business, have grown since he has become active on Facebook and other social media networking sites. These business relationships represent a range of connections, from those he never sees in person to those who have become close friends. Says Frick: "I have some people who I am friendly with and have online relationships with that I have never met. I have friendships I developed through the social sites but I have never met in person before that. We communicate via the sites regularly but for some, picking them out of a room full of people might be a challenge. I also have befriended people online via friends of Facebook friends and those friendships have sometimes turned into much closer relationships as well."

Frick echoed the cautionary note about social media networking site being just one more way of interacting but not a replacement for getting together in person when he concludes, "Even social media can't fully replace the value of interacting face-to-face with someone. At the base level, we need that. We, as humans, we need to connect with each other in person. All the webware in the world can't take the place of that at the end of the day."

TWITTER.COM

Dr. Wright, mentioned earlier in the book, is a chiropractor who now works fulltime on her cable show about entrepreneurism. She is also a twitter enthusiast. Says Wright: "I have used twitter for the best business results." She applauds the 140 characters that those who "tweet" on twitter are allowed to fill with any one post: "It's really almost training people for the media because they've got these short sound bytes to put out." At the point President Obama was inaugurated and he was forced to stop posting to his twitter.com account, he had more than 300,000 followers on twitter. Senator John McCain started posting at twitter.com in February 2009, which increased to more 125,000 followers just a month later.

Lola Augustus Brown, a Canadian-based parent and writer, is another twitter enthusiast. Brown says that twitter has helped her grow her relationships and her business. On twitter, almost 90% of those she connects to are strangers. By contrast, on Facebook, almost 90% are friends with whom she has a preexisting relationship. But Brown has made friends through twitter including another Canadian writer who lives two hours away. As a busy single mother, Brown probably would not had the time to connect with her, except for twitter.

Brown offers this piece of advice for those who want to grow their business relationships on twitter: do not be so focused on selling and your business or people will "un"-follow you. She recommends: "For every four posts you put on twitter, only one should be on business; the rest about your life."

Arizona-based Martin Zwilling of StartupProfessionals.com, who helps entrepreneurs with their business plans and does mentoring, is an excellent example of using twitter.com in the service of your business and business relationship goals. Zwilling directs his twitter followers to his startupprofessionals.com blog or newsletter, and vice versa. The results have been impressive with Zwilling growing his twitter followers (his twitter name is StartupPro) in just a year-and-a-half to over 250,000!

HOW SOCIAL NETWORKING SITES CAN HELP YOU GET A JOB

Here's an ideal example of how LinkedIn can lead to a job. Jan Wallen, who has written a book about LinkedIn, shared this example with me. It relates to her husband who decided it was important to get on LinkedIn since his wife is an expert on it. Jan's husband used to work at Wang Industries as a technology expert. He left that job to become a designer of customized furniture. So when he went on LinkedIn, the first person he linked to was someone with whom he worked at Wang. They communicated back and forth by e-mail and then they spoke on the phone. In the course of conversation, his friend mentioned that he and his wife wanted to get a new dining room table and chairs and they wanted one that was designed for them. Would he create their furniture? So his very first LinkedIn connection led to a paid job.

Ben Thompson, mentioned earlier in this chapter, shares this example of how LinkedIn helped him get a new client: "We had a design consultancy come in and pitch for a project where I was working at the time. I met the Founder/CEO of the company and received his business card. About 1.5 years later, as I was starting up my new company, I found him on LinkedIn, which was the start of an ongoing complementary relationship. He is based in St. Louis, and I now provide branding and graphic design consulting for his company from my studio in Los Angeles."

A 2002 *Wall Street Journal* article that quoted me discussing how friends were embarrassed about losing jobs and how some were retreating from their friends because they did not know what to say or how to socialize without the income to cover. At the time, I got an e-mail from someone named Chuck, who commented on my comments in the article. Recently, as I worked on this new book, I contacted Chuck again to see if he thought the situation was the same or if it had changed. He immediately wrote back, sharing with me the positive changes in this regard, developments he attributes it to the power of the social networking sites. As Chuck Tanowitz notes:

> In the past few years, I've seen quite a few people lose their jobs and gain new ones, but no one seems embarrassed by it. In fact, they talk about the search on their Facebook page or on their blog. They use it to their advantage, to a degree. On one level, it's another subject for them to talk about, but more importantly it's a way to reach out to their audience to find a new position. And people are very willing to help. In the past they may not have known who to call since they didn't have information available. Now they can look through their list and say, "Oh, Bob is looking for a position with a pharmaceutical company. I know a few people at pharmaceutical companies, and maybe I can link them."
>
> It's a very "pay it forward" kind of idea; people know that if they help Bob now, hopefully he can help them in the future. Yes, people understood this before, but the tools just

weren't there to make it happen. How do you call up someone with whom you haven't spoken in a while and say "I know a guy looking for a job in your area, any way you can help?" It had been an uncomfortable discussion. Now these same people follow you on Facebook or are connected with you on LinkedIn. That means they are, in a sense, opening themselves to the connections. Those tools break down the natural barrier to conversation and instead encourage it.

THE TIME-HONORED REFERRAL

There are ground rules about giving, or receiving, a referral that you might find useful to consider:

If You Are Providing a Referral

- If possible, only refer those with whom you have personally worked.
- If you don't have any firsthand experience with someone in the category that someone is searching for, be up front that this is just a name you are passing along but that you have no experience with this person.
- If you do have firsthand experience with someone and it was not a positive one, avoid making the referral by politely declining. Employees or contractors may say to you, when they finish a project or a job, "May I call on you for a recommendation?" This is your opportunity to be blunt about this. Say "yes" or "no." If it's yes, you might write a blanket "To Whom it May Concern" recommendation that you set aside, customizing it when the specific opportunity presents itself in the future. This could help you to be more specific about what this individual did that was positive since, months or years later, it may be harder to recall the kind of on-the-job details in the specific way that future employers will find most helpful. If your experience with someone was truly

negative, you can indicate that you would be an unwise choice for a reference.

If You Are Requesting a Referral
- Ask detailed questions about this person's experience with this individual.
- What was the nature of their association?
- What did you like or dislike about his or her performance?
- Was it worth whatever you paid for their services and/or their salary?
- Would you hire them again?
- Anything that could have gone better that might be useful to keep in mind if you do hire this person?
- Ask for a minimum of three names and their contact information as well as their background so you will ultimately be making the choice.
- Ask how he or she originally heard about this person: through a referral, how else?

Chapter Eleven

● ● ●

Moving Ahead and Summing Up

Strategy #57
Furthering Your Work Relationship Plan

Read some of the seminal or contemporary classic work relationships books, such as Dale Carnegie's *How to Win Friends and
Influence People*, first published in 1937 but still a bestseller today,
or marketing guru Keith Ferrazzi's *Never Eat Alone*. Check out
other books with the general theme of work relationships, such as
Ronna Lichtenberg, *It's Not Business, It's Personal*, negative ones,
such as *Toxic Workplace* by Mitchell Kusy and Elizabeth
Holloway or Robert I. Sutton's *The No Asshole Rule*, or focus on a
specific aspect of work relationships, such as Carol Kinsey
Goman's *The Nonverbal Advantage* or Milo Frank's *Get Your
Point Across in 30 Seconds*.

Go to workshops on work relationships. If you cannot take
the time to go in person, take a webinar or hire a work
relationship coach if you could use help in this area. If you are
already seeing a therapist or counselor, if you are still having
challenges in this area, make sure you're discussing work
relationships in your sessions and not just personal friends or
family connections.

CREATING A WORK RELATIONSHIPS PLAN

At the beginning of this book, I recommended that you
answer twenty questions about your current work relationships in
the "Office or Business Relationship Self-Quiz." Refer back to

those questions and to your answers. Now take that test again and see where your answers are different since you have read this book.

Based on a review of your answers to those questions, and your self-analysis of your work relationships, use this opportunity to create a work relationships plan for the next week, month, year, and five years. Ask, and answer, such questions as: Who will you try to meet, or reconnect with, at your company, or at other companies, in your industry or in your community that could help your career? If there is someone you work with, or for, and the relationship is unsatisfactory, how will you try to turn the situation around?

Make sure you get to know all the people you work with on a regular basis and prioritize developing, or enhancing, a positive relationship with your coworkers, bosses, vendors, clients, customers, or subordinates. Putting together a work relationship plan, just as you would make a list of work project goals that you want to accomplish, may help you to achieve that goal. Therefore, on a separate piece of paper, write down your answers to these questions:

- Over the next five days, what work relationships will I try to develop, or reinforce?
- Over the next month, what work relationships will I try to develop, or reinforce?
- Within three months, who are at least three movers and shakers at my company that I will try to meet and/or get to know better?
- Within nine months, who are at least ten movers and shakers in my industry that I will try to meet and/or get to know better?
- By the end of the year, what are the associations that I am part of that I will have stepped up my active participation through volunteering to be on a committee, writing for

their newsletter, reaching out to at least half a dozen other members, or other ways of improving the relationship value of that membership?

- What are the professional activities I am involved in? How many people do I know through those activities? If I need to get to know more individuals, how will I accomplish that goal?

- Make a list of the top 100 professional relationships you have that are the core of your work relationships network. If you lack 100, start from whatever number you do have and devise a plan to add new key relationships to your professional circle, one person at a time.

Even if you started out five or ten years ago with a strong business network, you have to assess and reassess your network on at least an annual basis. Business associates move to different companies, bonds are diminished, people retire, others move away or move on, or even pass on. Feelings can change and relationships, if not attended to, can diminish in strength and concern.

Summing Up

As Michael Hughes, Canadian networking expert, puts it: "At LinkedIn and Facebook I have access to 4.3 million people. It's ludicrous when you have access to that many people when you're already getting 200 e-mails a day and when you're bombarded with requests for your time and for your attention. It loses its impact."

So what are the relationship challenges we all face today? Canadian social networking expert Hughes says: "How do we choose *who* we are going to respond to? The need for us to filter the right connections is a priority. The human dynamic is more important today than it has ever been because of all the choices we have. Business skills, relationship skills, and interpersonal skills are the cornerstone strategies for success. This is a huge shift for many people who have never seen it in those terms. My network is important to me. It has opportunities, it has options, it has resources, and it has insights."

Unfortunately, each of us is bombarded by so many requests on a daily, even a minute by minute basis; there are just too many requests to connect, or requests for information, that fall through the cracks. But it is not just a request that falls through the cracks; it is also a human being, a person, a potential advocate, mentor, fan, or partner. You may think that others forget that you never returned their call or that you failed to respond to a request. But do you forget if it happens to you? When you do it to others, have you turned a total stranger into a potential "bad-mouther," or a current advocate into someone who is lukewarm toward you or even negative about you because of your seeming indifference? Is there another way to handle it, perhaps with an auto responder or having virtual assistants or college interns for credit who can help you get caught up on e-mails, phone calls, or correspondence?

Who has the time for all this connecting and socializing when there's work to be done! Alas, whether it's in our personal lives or at work or in our careers, having relationships that are positive, nurturing, and stimulating is a big part of the work. But not everyone sees it that way. I remember when I did a presentation on work relationships at an IT company. Before the session began, I went around the room, talking to some of the consultants who were enjoying the free pizza that management gave out as part of the lunchtime presentation. This particular consultant, when I asked how his work relationships were, confided that he got to work by 4:30 in the morning, when there were few, if any, other workers there, so he could do what he had to do and leave as soon as possible, so he could avoid his coworkers. Instead of seeing his coworkers as a source of inspiration, motivation, and fun, he saw them as individuals to be avoided.

But look at others whose companies were founded because of strong relationships such as computer giant Microsoft, founded by childhood friends Bill Gates and Paul Allen; ice cream entrepreneurs and school friends Ben and Jerry; as well as such famous bands as music legends the Beatles and the Rolling Stones.

Or what about the ten coworkers at the insurance company in Whitehouse Station, New Jersey who each spent $5 so their coworker could then buy them fifty $1 lottery tickets? Bob Space sent a memo to his nine co-workers and in it he wrote: "We won the big one!" The ten coworkers had won the $216 million Mega Millions jackpot which converted into $140 million after taxes, or $14 million for each coworker.

If winning the lottery with your coworkers seems a bit farfetched, maybe at least having a coworker who is a friend, even a casual friend, is less dependent on just luck and more within your reach. Think about that line from Frank Capra's classic 1946 movie, *It's a Wonderful Life*, uttered by Clarence, the angel sent down from heaven to help George Bailey see that he did matter even though Bailey believes that his company has lost everything financially: "Remember no man is a failure who has friends."

You have learned 57 different strategies for improving your work connections. You probably have one or more strategies that are your favorites, or that speak most to you and your particular situation. It may depend on your personality, the type of job you have, or what else is going on in your life at this time.

Here, in summary, are ten top work relationship strategies:

Strategy #1: Create a Favorable First Impression: In-Person, over the Phone and through E-Mail

Strategy #6: Dealing with Negative Personality Types

Strategy #7: Form Relationships with Positive Types

Strategy #14: Find a Way to Motivate Others to Want to Get Along with You

Strategy #27: Reexamine Your Attitude Toward Conflict

Strategy #31: Deal with the "Back-Off" before it turns Antagonistic

Strategy #51: Benefit From Harsh Feedback About Your Work

Strategy #52: Using Meditation to Reduce Stress

Strategy #53: Adios (Saying *Good-bye if Leaving is the Best Option*)

Strategy #56: Use Social Networking to Improve Your Work Relationships

"Most of business is about people," says Ken Ross, founder and CEO of an online forum for CEOs called Expert CEO. "It's not just having the right skills," continues Ross. "It's being able to relate or interact with people, working effectively with coworkers/peers, subordinates, and your boss. For CEOs, it's about hiring the right people and keeping them motivated."

To succeed in business, you have to succeed with people. Yes, a friend or two at work or in business would be nice and hopefully you have that ideal or, if you do not, this book has helped you to come closer to achieving that, if that is your goal. But at work and in business, for most of us, friendship is not required. What is necessary is mutual respect as well as a strong, positive connection to your coworkers, boss, employees, clients, customers, or service providers, whether you work in an office together or you work from home and connect over the Internet, whether you are a 22-year-old just starting out at your first job or a 61-year-old reentering the work force because your early retirement had to come to an abrupt end. Those 40 to 80 hours that you put in at work each and every week except when you are able to get some time off for holidays or for summer or winter vacations will be a lot more fulfilling, stimulating, productive, and less stressful if you have constructive and responsive work relationships you can count on.

Our earnings may pay the bills, but it is the positive relationships we form through work that last in our hearts forever.

Selected Bibliography

Bailey, Simon T. *Release Your Brilliance*. NY: HarperCollins, 2007.

Bureau of Labor Statistics, United States Department of Labor. "News," "Survey of Workplace Violence Prevention, 2005," released October 27, 2006.

Carnegie, Dale. *How to Win Friends and Influence People*. New York: Simon & Schuster, Inc., Pocket Books, 1937, 1964.

_____. *Dale Carnegie's Scrapbook: A Treasury of the Wisdom of the Ages*. Edited, with a selection of Dale Carnegie's own writings, by Dorothy Carnegie. Hauppauge, NY: Dale Carnegie & Associates, Inc., 1959.

Couric, Katie. Interview with Captain Chesley "Sully" Sullenberger, *CBS 60 Minutes*, Sunday, February 8, 2009.

Ferrazzi, Keith. *Who's Got Your Back?* New York: Broadway Business, 2009.

_____ with Tahl Raz. *Never Eat Alone*. New York: Doubleday, 2005.

Frank, Milo O. *How to Get Your Point Across in 30 Seconds or Less*. New York: Simon & Schuster, Inc., Pocket Books, 1986.

Gardner, Robert A. "Preventing Workplace Violence: Management Considerations." *The California Labor Letter*, August 1993, pages 8-1l.

Gladwell, Malcolm. *The Tipping Point*. New York: Penguin (Back Bay Books), 2002.

Gabor, Don. *How to Start a Conversation and Make Friends*. Revised edition. New York: Simon & Schuster, Inc., Fireside Books, 2001.

Goman, Carol Kinsey. *The Nonverbal Advantage*. San Francisco: Berrett-Kohler, 2008.

_____. "The Truth about Liars." Blog posted at http://www.communitelligence.com, January 26, 2009.

Goodman, Michelle. "As Workers Get Ax, Friendships Also Cut." January 8, 2009, http://www.abcnews.go.com

Gurchiek, Kathy. *HR Magazine,* "Bullying: It's Not Just on the Playground." June 2005, page 40-41.

Hall, Edward. *The Hidden Dimension.* New York: Anchor Books, 1990.

————. *The Silent Language.* New York: Anchor Books, 1973.

Hallinan, Joseph. *Why We Make Mistakes.* New York: Broadway Books, 2009.

Hodgkinson, Tom. "With Friends Like These…" *The Guardian* (United Kingdom), January 14, 2008.

Hsieh, Tony. *Delivering Happiness: A Path to Profits, Passion and Purpose.* New York: Business One (Hachette), 2010.

Hymowitz, Carol. "Women Get Better at Forming Networks to Help Their Climb." *Wall Street Journal,* November 19, 2007, page B1.

Jamieson, Alastair. "Long hours put workers at risk of dementia, according to research into damage to brain." telegraph.co.uk/health/healthnews/4803218/Long-hours-put-workers-at-risk-of…2/28/2009.

Jansen, Julie. *You Want Me to Work With Who?* New York: Penguin, 2006.

Kawasaki, Guy. "Ten Ways to Use Linkedin." http://www.blog.linkedin.com/blog July 25, 2007.

Kiely, Kathy, "Obama's Connections, from Trait to Train." *USA Today,* Friday, January 16, 2009, page 5A.

Kusy, Mitchell and Elixabeth Holloway. *Toxic Workplace! Managing Toxic Personalities and Their Systems of Power.* San Francisco: Jossey-Bass (Wiley), 2009.

Lavington, Camille with Stephanie Losee. *You've Only Got Three Seconds.* New York: Doubleday, 1997.

Leck, Joanne D. and Bella L. Galperin. "Worker Responses to Bully Bosses." *Canadian Public Policy/Analysa de Politiques,* Vol. XXXII, No. 1, 2006, pages 85-97.

Lichtenberg, Ronna. *It's Not Business, It's Personal.* New York: Hyperion, 2002.

Linkow, Peter R. "Managing Across Language, Culture, Time, and Location." New York: The Conference Board, 2008.

Lynch, Jennifer and Deborah Katz. "Beyond ADR: Integrated Conflict Management Systems," PowerPoint presentation.

Mehrabian, Albert. *Nonverbal Communication.* Aldine-Atherton, Illinois: Chicago, 1972.

_____. *Silent Messages*, Wadsworth, California: Belmont, 1971.

Montaigne. "Of Friendship" in *The Complete Essays of Montaigne*, pages 135-44, edited and translated by Donald M. Frame. Stanford, CA: Stanford University Press, 1958.

"No Doubts: Women Are Better Managers." Corner Office: Carol Smith. *New York Times*, July 26, 2009, page 2.

Ruben, Brent D. and Lea P. Stewart. *Communication and Human Behavior* (5th edition). Boston, MA: Allyn & Bacon, 2005.

Sorkin, Andrew Ross. "Dealbook: Real Losses Have Nothing to Do With Money." *New York Times*, Sunday, October 21, 2007, page 8.

Sutton, Robert I. *The No Asshole* Rule: Building a Civilized Workplace and Surviving One That Isn't. New York: Business Plus, 2007.

Tulgan, Bruce. *Not Everybody Gets a Trophy: How to Manage Generation Y.* New York: Wiley/Jossey-Bass, 2009.

Wilson, Craig. "Mistakes are like passwords: We all make 'em." *USA Today*, February 11, 2009, page D1.

Yager, Jan. *Business Protocol.* New York: Wiley, 1991; 2nd edition, Stamford, CT: Hannacroix Creek Books, Inc., 2001.

_____. *Making Your Office Work for You.* Garden City, New York: Doubleday, 1989.

_____. *Friendshifts: The Power of Friendship and How It Shapes Our Lives.* Stamford, CT: Hannacroix Creek Books, 2nd editon, 1999.

_____. *When Friendship Hurts: How to Deal With Friends Who Betray, Abandon, or Wound You.* New York: Simon & Schuster, Inc., Fireside Books, 2002.

_____. *Who's That Sitting at My Desk? Workship, Friendship, or Foe?* Stamford, CT: Hannacroix Creek Books, Inc., 2004.

_____. *Work Less, Do More: The 14-Day Productivity Makeover.* New York: Sterling Publishing Co., Inc., 2008.

Resources

● ● ●

BUSINESS AND SOCIAL NETWORKING ONLINE SITES

Social networking sites that are being used to generate business, create new relationships, or stay in contact with current or previous coworkers or business relationships

www.linkedin.com	www.facebook.com
www.twitter.com	www.myspace.com
www.plaxo.com	www.xing.com
www.classmates.com	www.hi5.com

ORGANIZATIONS, COMPANIES, OR ASSOCIATIONS WITH IN-PERSON NETWORKING

CEO Club
http://www.ceoclubs.org

Mediabistro.com
http://www.mediabistro.com

NETWORKING EVENTS FOR THOSE IN THE MEDIA IN SEVERAL MAJOR U.S. CITIES AND INTERNATIONALLY

National Association for Female Executives (NAFE)
http://www.nafe.org

National Association of Women Business Owners (NAWBO)
http://www.nawbo.org
Women's Media Group
http://www.womensmediagroup.org

Australia
Women's Network Australia Pty Ltd
PO Box 1723,
Sunnybank Hills,
QLD Australia 4109.
http://www.womensnetwork.com.au

Conflict Resolution
American Arbitration Association
1633 Broadway, 10th Floor
New York, New York 10019
http://www.adr.org

Association for Conflict Resolution (ACR)
5151 Wisconsin Avenue, NW, Suite 500
Washington, DC 20016
http://www.acrnet.org

There are 22 regional chapters throughout the United States.

Workplace Bullying
Websites and organizations offering help with workplace bullying
The Workplace Bully Institute, WBI
P.O. Box 29915
Bellingham, WA 98228
www.workplacebullying.org

Work Trauma
P.O. Box 2873
Wilropark, 1731
Roodepoort, South Africa
http://www.worktrauma.org

Index

About the Author

●　●　●

Jan Yager, Ph.D. has been researching, writing, speaking, and coaching about work and work relationships for more than two decades. She has a Ph.D. in sociology from The City University of New York Graduate Center and is the prolific author of 30 award-winning books on a variety of work/business/career and relationship and other topics including victims of crime, which have been translated into 24 languages, including *Business Protocol; Work Less, Do More: The 14-Day Productivity Makeover; Career Opportunities in the Publishing Industry; Career Opportunities in the Film Industry; Who's That Sitting at My Desk? Workship, Friends, or Foe?; Making Your Office Work For You; When Friendship Hurts; Friendshifts; Victims;* and others.

　　Jan's been interviewed on major TV and radio shows as well as in newspaper, magazine, and online publications including *Oprah, The View, Today Show, The Early Show, Good Morning America, Nightline, Sunday Morning,* CNN, the *New York Times,* the *Wall Street Journal,* Forbes.com, aol.com, cnn.com, and others. She has taught at several universities including Penn State, the New York Institute of Technology, the New School and, most recently, the University of Connecticut. For more information, go to:

www.drjanyager.com.
On twitter: www.twitter.com/drjanyager

To contact Dr. Yager, send an e-mail to: jyager@aol.com or write to:

Dr. Jan Yager
1127 High Ridge Road, #110
Stamford, Connecticut 06905 USA